the accidental vegetarian

the accidental vegetarian

Delicious food without meat

Simon Rimmer

MITCHELL BEAZLEY

This book is dedicated to Ali, Flo, and Hamish

This edition published for Indigo Books & Music Inc.

Photographs by Jason Lowe
Designed by Simon Daley
Edited by Barbara Dixon and Victoria Alers-Hankey

ISBN 978-1-8453-3747-6

Manufactured in China

2 4 6 8 10 9 7 5 3 1

Contents

Introduction	6
Dips and morsels	8
Salads	22
Small platefuls	38
Big platefuls	62
Side dishes	98
Desserts	108
Index	142

Introduction

When I bought Greens in 1990 I had two cookery books, a bank loan and no idea how to cook! The plan was that I and Simon Connolly, my business partner, would swan around as the hosts with the most, drinking nice wine and chatting up women while someone else cooked and we coined it in, big-style. That was until we worked out the size of our bank loan and the cost of employing a chef—so we became the chefs.

Simon and I met while working as waiters in the Steak and Kebab restaurant in Manchester, England. It was a brilliant place to work, full of people waiting to do other things—act, write, fly to the moon—but all loving the buzz of the place. Let me tell you something about the restaurant industry, the hours seem unsociable to you, but there isn't a more sociable job in the world. You work hard, meet great people and then sit down at the end of the shift and have a few glasses with your mates.

From there I'd got the restaurant bug, so we decided to open our own place. At the time it didn't matter what sort of restaurant it was as long as it was cheap. I had always had my eye on Greens, then one morning I drove past it and saw a "For Sale" sign being put outside. It was too good to resist and after much negotiation we became the proud owners of a veggie cafe.

I should point out here that we were, and still are, carnivores, so looking through veggie cookbooks in 1990, and being confronted with brown, stodgy food that was all a little bit worthy, was not fun. So we opened with such "classics" as nut roast, vegetarian lasagne, and some dreadful generic curry—you don't have to tell me how awful it sounds.

It was chaos at the start. We had no idea how to organize our preparation and purchasing and we were working 100 hours a week for practically nothing. I hated everything we were cooking, but we were improving.

Surprisingly, we were busy; while the food left a lot to be desired, we were overtly friendly and working very hard. I'd caught the food bug; I was determined to make veggie food more exciting, to get people to eat at Greens because the food was good. I consumed cookery books, learnt techniques, researched cultures who have great vegetarian dishes—Asian, Mediterranean, African—and tried to use French and Italian techniques alongside them; I was extremely experimental and obsessed.

After two years I was getting there; the restaurant was full and the food had become unique. I sourced unusual suppliers of fruit and veg to bring exotics to the table, I looked for different pasta makers and vegetarian cheese suppliers and I made sure that the still popular generic "vegetable" term never appeared on the menu.

After thirteen years I still love Greens. It feels like home. Our customers are very protective of it, they don't like change, or the fact that they can't always get a table—we reckon we turn away 400 people a week, which is quite amazing, so if you fancy coming, book early!

I think my food is best described as magpie cuisine—I'll steal an idea from anywhere, combining an Asian curry with Jamaican rice and peas. I always try to let the availability of ingredients influence the menus: strawberry soups in summer, Italian bean and Parmesan-roasted parsnips in winter, crisp radish and watercress salads in May.

The recipes in this book are both attainable and inspiring. I don't have formal training as a chef, so I've learnt by the seat of my pants. It hasn't been easy, but it's been a fantastic journey and I'm still learning—so what are you waiting for, turn the pages and get cooking!

Dips and morsels

Feta cheese bread

There's something really satisfying about making bread—watching it rise, kneading the dough and, best of all, eating warm bread that you've made for yourself. This bread is so delicious, all you need with it is extra-virgin olive oil and some pickled chiles.

1 Dissolve the yeast and sugar in a little of the water. This takes about 5 minutes.

2 Tip the flour and salt onto a work surface and make a well in the center. Add the rest of the water and the now frothy yeast mix and mix to a dough. Knead for 7–8 minutes until it stops being sticky—the dough is ready when it will stretch out between your hands without breaking.

3 Put the dough into an oiled bowl, cover and leave to double in size—at least 2 hours.

4 Turn the dough out onto a lightly floured surface and "knock back"—to get all the puffiness out of it.

5 Knead the oil, cheese, mint, and pepper into the dough, divide into four pieces and mold each into a round loaf. Put on a buttered and floured baking sheet, cover with a damp cloth and leave to rise at room temperature for 40–60 minutes.

6 Preheat the oven to 350°F. Glaze the loaves with egg wash and bake for around 30–40 minutes. Leave to cool.

½oz (2 sachets) instant yeast

1 tsp superfine sugar

2½ cups warm water

2¼lb strong bread flour, plus extra for dusting

2 tbsp salt

4 tbsp extra-virgin olive oil, plus extra for greasing

12oz feta cheese, crumbled

handful of freshly chopped mint leaves

freshly ground black pepper

butter, for greasing

1 egg, beaten, for eggwash

Blinis with sour cream and roasted bell peppers

Makes 15

The joy of blinis is that they're dead versatile—top them with sweet, savory or a combination of the two. Have them for breakfast, lunch or supper, make them big or small. Use your imagination for the toppings.

1 First make the blinis. Sift the flours and a little salt into a bowl. Make a well in the center and add the two whole eggs and one egg white.

2 Mix together the yeast, sugar, and milk and leave for a couple of minutes. Pour this slowly into the flour mix and whisk to make a smooth batter. Stir in the butter.

3 Cover the batter and leave in a warm place for 1 hour.

4 Meanwhile, make the topping. Roast or char the peppers until the skin is blackened. Put them in a plastic bag, seal and let them go cold, when the skin will fall away. Seed the peppers and cut into wide strips.

5 Just before cooking the blinis, whisk the remaining egg white and fold into the batter.

6 Heat a little oil in a skillet. Pour enough batter into the pan to make a 4inch blini. When the batter bubbles up, flip it over and cook the other side. Keep the blini warm while you make the rest of the pancakes in the same way.

7 Spoon some sour cream onto each blini and top with some of the pepper pieces, an olive, and a twist of black pepper.

*If using dried yeast, follow the maker's instructions for quantity and use.

$1\frac{1}{2}$ cups buckwheat or wholemeal flour

$1\frac{3}{4}$ cups all-purpose flour

2 whole eggs, plus 2 egg whites

$1\frac{3}{4}$oz fresh yeast*

2 tsp superfine sugar

3 cups warm milk

1 tbsp melted butter

vegetable oil for frying

salt

For the topping

4 red bell peppers

1 cup set sour cream

15 black Ascoloni olives

freshly ground black pepper

Spicy red bell pepper hummus with coriander seed flat bread

Feeds 6

I thought long and hard about putting hummus in the book, it's the kind of thing that you expect from a veggie cookbook—but this is different! Firstly, the hummus is lovely and garlicky, it's also lemony and it's got a great little kick at the end from the peppers. Making breads can be hit and miss at times, which is why I love making flat breads—you have a little more margin for error, plus they have a delicious taste and texture.

1 Start with the bread. Dry-fry the coriander seeds, then lightly crush them in a mortar and pestle. Don't turn them into a powder, but also don't leave them tooth-breaking size. Put them into a pan with the water and bring just to a boil.

2 Put the yogurt into a bowl and add the yeast. Pour the coriander seeds and water into the bowl and stir well.

3 Add 1½ cups of the flour, and use your hands to combine it well, then cover the bowl and leave to prove for 25 minutes. Contrary to popular belief, it doesn't have to be somewhere warm, but it helps.

4 After the proving, turn the dough out onto a lightly floured surface, add the salt, oil, and remaining flour and give this a really good mix. Put back in the bowl, cover and leave to prove again for 1 hour, when it should have just about doubled in size.

5 Turn the dough out onto a lightly floured surface and knock it back. Divide the dough into six, then roll into little balls. Roll each ball out to 4–5inch circles.

6 To cook the bread, brush each circle of dough with a little oil and cook for about 30 seconds on each side, either in a shallow skillet or on a griddle pan. Put a cooked flat bread on each plate.

7 For the hummus, put all the ingredients except the oil, olives, and fresh chile in the blender and whiz until smooth. With the motor running, add a stream of oil to loosen the mixture. Turn out into a dish, garnish with the olives and chargrilled chile and serve with the coriander seed flat bread.

15oz can chickpeas (garbanzo beans), drained and rinsed

4 garlic cloves

¼ cup tahini paste

juice of 3 lemons

3½oz sweet pickled chile peppers

olive oil to loosen

salt and freshly ground black pepper

6 olives and 1 red chile, charred or griddled, to serve

For the coriander seed flat bread

1 tsp coriander seeds

½ cup water

1–1¼ cups plain yogurt

1½ tsp dried yeast

5 cups bread flour, plus extra for dusting

1 tbsp salt

2 tbsp vegetable oil, plus extra for brushing

Fried halloumi with lemon and capers

Feeds 4

You'll not see halloumi on a cheeseboard, because raw it tastes a bit like plastic, but when dusted with spiced flour and fried it becomes a right tasty morsel. After that the zingy lemon dressing cuts through the sweetness of the cheese to perfection. Mop up the dressing with my feta cheese bread (see page 10), or a slab of crusty white if that's what you've got.

1 Combine the flour with the cayenne and season well. Dust each slice of cheese with the flour.

2 Heat some oil in a skillet until hot, then fry the halloumi for about 1 minute on each side, until golden.

3 To make the dressing, put the lemon juice, vinegar, garlic, and mustard into a bowl and whisk together. Keep whisking and slowly add the oil, a little at a time. Season to taste, then add the capers and herbs.

4 Sit two pieces of cheese on each plate (it looks good on top of some peppery watercress) and drizzle with the dressing.

$3\frac{1}{2}$ tbsp all-purpose flour
1 tsp cayenne pepper
8oz halloumi cheese, cut into 8 slices
vegetable oil for frying
salt and freshly ground black pepper
watercress, to serve (optional)

For the dressing

juice of 1 lemon
1 tbsp white wine vinegar
1 garlic clove, crushed
1 tsp Dijon mustard
3 tbsp extra-virgin olive oil
$1\frac{1}{2}$ tsp capers in vinegar
freshly chopped parsley
freshly chopped cilantro

Sticky rice and peanut balls

The ultimate beer snack. Be very careful, these little beasts are addictive: Thai spices, peanuts, rice, and deep-fried—they're crying out for a beer.

1 Blend half the rice in a food processor until it's not quite a paste. Turn out into a bowl and combine this with the remaining rice, the curry paste, lime juice, and salt to taste. Mix it up really well.

2 Roll the mixture into balls 1–1½ inches in diameter. Now roll the balls in the peanuts and deep-fry in hot oil until golden. Drain on paper towels and serve with chili sauce.

2¼ cups cooked Thai jasmine rice
4 tbsp red Thai curry paste
juice of 1 lime
1 cup roasted peanuts, finely crushed
vegetable oil for deep-frying
salt
sweet chili sauce for dipping

Favetta

Feeds 4

This is such a lovely dish whether you are a veggie or not. You can use frozen beans, but fresh ones are so much better. Serve with coriander seed flat bread (see page 12) or with some roasted vegetables.

1 Blanch the beans in boiling water for 2 minutes, maximum, then plunge into really ice-cold water. Drain the beans and peel off the hard outer skins.

2 Put the beans, thyme, garlic, and lemon juice in a blender and pulse until smooth.

3 With the motor running, pour in enough of the oil to blend until it's the consistency of hummus.

4 Turn out into a bowl and season.

400g/14oz fresh fava beans
handful of fresh thyme
1 garlic clove
juice of 1 lemon
½ cup extra-virgin olive oil
salt and freshly ground black pepper

Tomato and mozzarella cakes

Feeds 6

Each cake is a tomato risotto filled with melting cheese. You may have eaten the little round versions of these called "arancini," or little oranges. These larger versions could make a great lunch with simply dressed arugula.

1 Melt the butter in a heavy-bottom pan. Add the rice and cook for a couple of minutes on a low heat. When the rice starts to become a little translucent around the edges, add the wine and cook for another minute.

2 Add a ladleful of warm stock (it must be warm to enable the rice to cook properly). When the stock has been absorbed, add another ladleful and continue doing this until all the stock has been added and/or the rice is tender.

3 Next, fold in the sun-dried tomatoes and the cream and season well. Leave the rice to cool.

4 Divide the rice into six and roll into balls. The rice will be nice and sticky. Make a hole in the center of each ball and press some of the cheese into it. Cover with the rice and flatten into a patty shape.

5 Roll the patties in flour, then egg, then breadcrumbs, and deep-fry at 350°F. You don't want the oil to be too hot or the outside will cook and the middle will be cold. Fry till crisp and golden, then drain on paper towels and serve with dressed arugula leaves.

½ stick butter

2 cups arborio rice, rinsed and drained

splash of white wine

3½ cups warm stock

3½oz sun-dried tomatoes, chopped

splash of cream

1½ cups cubed mozzarella cheese

all-purpose flour, for rolling

1 egg, beaten

2½–3 cups fresh breadcrumbs

vegetable oil for deep-frying

dressed arugula leaves, to serve

Thai spiced potato cakes
with spicy coleslaw

Makes 8 cakes

I first went to Thailand in 1996 and I found it so inspiring—it's a food lover's delight. I'd always loved Thai food—green curries, pad-thai, sticky rice—with all their beautiful fragrances. When you're there, the smell of lime leaves, lemon grass, coconut, and charring chiles you get from the excellent street food stalls is overwhelming. So this fantastic little morsel will give you a spicy, fragrant taste of the East. If you can't get fresh lime leaves, then use dried, but the smell of fresh makes it worth a trail around the stores. You should have tingly lips from the chiles and the wasabi in the coleslaw —don't go easy on them, live on the edge.

1 First, make the potato cakes. Put the mashed and grated potatoes in a large bowl, add all the other potato cake ingredients and season.

2 Mold the mixture into eight 3inch rounds, about 1inch thick (or make sixteen mini-cakes—great for parties), and pop them into the fridge for about 1 hour.

3 Set up three plates or bowls: one with flour, one with eggwash, and one with the breadcrumbs. First roll the cakes in flour, dust off any excess, then roll them in the egg and finally in the breadcrumbs.

4 You can shallow- or deep-fry them (I find that deep-frying gives a crisper texture). If you shallow-fry, be careful not to burn them—a gentle heat is best. Either way, they're done when crisp and golden.

5 Put a spoonful of coleslaw on each plate and sit a potato cake on top. Sprinkle some chopped cilantro over and add a wedge of lime on the side—and don't forget to pour yourself a nice cold glass of Singha beer.

all-purpose flour, for rolling

2 eggs, beaten, for eggwash

2½–3 cups fresh breadcrumbs

vegetable oil for frying

1 quantity spicy coleslaw, to serve (see page 32)

freshly chopped cilantro and lime wedges, to serve

For the potato cakes

3 large mealy potatoes, say russets, peeled, cooked and mashed

1 raw potato, peeled and grated

3 tbsp mayonnaise

1 bunch of scallions, finely chopped

2 small red chiles, seeded and chopped

freshly chopped cilantro

2 garlic cloves, crushed

2 stalks of lemon grass, finely chopped

4 kaffir lime leaves, finely chopped

1inch piece of fresh ginger, finely chopped

1 tsp ground cinnamon

2 shallots, finely chopped

salt and freshly ground black pepper

Norimaki
sushi rolls

Feeds 6

Hands up if you thought "sushi" meant raw fish? Quite a lot of you I reckon. Well, I did too, but it actually means vinegared rice, so with that piece of knowledge you can make these delicious, healthy nori rolls and show off to friends and family about the true meaning of sushi. Nori is roasted and rolled seaweed and comes in sheets.

1 Put the rice in a pan with the water and bring to a boil. Cover and simmer for 5 minutes, then take off the heat, leave covered and allow to cool.

2 When the rice is cool, put it in a bowl, season and add the sugar and vinegar. Mix well.

3 Lay out the nori sheets and spread a little wasabi on each. Put a line, about 1inch wide, of rice a little way in from the bottom edge.

4 Press some cucumber and pepper into the rice. Top with more rice and roll up tightly. Chill for 30 minutes, then cut into 1½inch long pieces. Cut off and discard the uneven ends.

5 Make a dipping sauce by heating the vinegar, sugar, and chile until the sugar dissolves.

6 Serve the sushi rolls with the dipping sauce, extra wasabi paste, soy sauce, and pickled red ginger.

¾ **cup sushi rice, rinsed thoroughly and drained**

1 cup water

2 tbsp sugar

3½ tbsp rice wine vinegar

4 sheets dried nori

wasabi paste

½ **cucumber, peeled, seeded, and cut into batons**

½ **red bell pepper, seeded, and cut into batons**

salt

soy sauce and pickled red ginger, to serve

For the dipping sauce

½ **cup rice vinegar**

6 tbsp sugar

1 small red chile, finely chopped

Patatas bravas

In Spain these are made by deep-frying the potatoes, salting them and squeezing a spicy tomato "ketchup" over them. But this is the yummiest way to do it—slowly roasting the potatoes with chiles. I like to make them a day in advance so the olive oil, chiles, and tomatoes can really get to work on the potato. Whenever we have a party at home I make a bucket-load of these—they do go so well with a cold beer.

1 Preheat the oven to 425ºF. Heat a load of oil in a massive roasting pan until really hot. Cut the potatoes into 1inch cubes. Chuck away any uneven bits, so you're left with neat shapes, they look nicer.

2 Throw the potatoes in the oil and give them a little shake. Season well, then pop into the oven for about 10 minutes until they begin to brown.

3 Add the tomatoes, chiles, and garlic and stir well. Cook for another 25–35 minutes until the potatoes are soft on the inside, but with a little bit of crispness outside.

4 Either add the parsley and serve, or leave them until the next day, then reheat, adding more oil, and add the parsley before eating.

5 If you're making these for a party, put a load in a secret place for yourself, you know it makes sense.

lots of olive oil

1½lb 5oz russet or Yukon Gold potatoes, peeled

2 cups canned chopped tomatoes

3 red chiles, chopped

4 garlic cloves, crushed

lots of freshly chopped parsley

salt and freshly ground black pepper

Dolmades

Makes 20

Whenever I'm in Greece I can't stop eating these little fellas. There's loads of different varieties—meaty, herby, veggie, and these, which have golden raisins and pine nuts. Serving them with yummy tzatziki is essential.

1 Heat the oil in a pan and fry the shallots and garlic until soft. Add the rice, golden raisins, pine nuts, and lemon juice and fry for 1 minute. Season, then add the water.

2 Cover the pan and simmer for 15 minutes, then turn off the heat and leave to cool.

3 Once the mixture is cool, add the scallions, mint, and parsley.

4 Rinse the grape leaves in water, then place them shiny side down on a board. Put about 2 tsp of the cooled stuffing on each leaf and roll into a tight parcel. Chill until ready to eat.

5 For the tzatziki, mix the cucumber with the yogurt, garlic, mint, lemon juice, and seasoning. Tip into a serving bowl and top with a dash of olive oil.

6 You can serve the dolmades either cold or warm (just heat them in a steamer). Put them on a large plate with the tzatziki in the middle and get stuck in.

1 tbsp olive oil

3 shallots, finely chopped

2 garlic cloves, crushed

$2/3$ cup short-grain rice, rinsed and drained

$1/2$ cup golden raisins

$1/2$ cup pine nuts, toasted

juice of 1 lemon

$3/4$ cup water

1 bunch of scallions, finely chopped

handful of finely chopped fresh mint leaves and parsley

20 preserved grape leaves

salt and freshly ground black pepper

For the tzatziki

1 cucumber, peeled, seeded, and coarsely grated

$3/4$ cup Greek yogurt

4 garlic cloves, crushed

handful of freshly chopped mint leaves

juice of $1/2$ lemon

extra-virgin olive oil

Salads

Santa Fé Caesar salad

A good Caesar salad is a joy to behold, but unfortunately the rise of café bars has meant that a bit of romaine lettuce, soggy croûtons, mayo, and Parmesan are masquerading as the real thing. So here is a great salad, which has the strength of a Caesar with spicy bits of the Mexican border. Hail Caesar-Gringo!

1 To make the dressing, put the mayonnaise, mustard, and garlic into a bowl and whisk in the lime juice and vinegar. Mix in the grated Parmesan and season to taste.

2 To make up the salad, cut the lettuce into 1–2inch wide slices, chuck away the bottom, and put the slices into a large bowl. Season with a little salt and pepper.

3 To make the croûtons, dry-fry the tortillas in a pan until a little charred, then break up into the lettuce bowl.

4 Chuck in the beans and chiles.

5 Add about half the dressing and toss, then add the rest (if you think it's dressed enough with half that's fine) and the avocado, shallots, and cilantro leaves.

6 Finally, top with some large Parmesan shavings (use a potato peeler to get the right effect) and serve.

1 romaine lettuce, trimmed

2 soft corn tortillas

½ cup cooked/canned pinto beans, or kidney beans, drained and rinsed

2 red chiles, seeded and chopped

1 ripe avocado, chopped

2 shallots, finely sliced

fresh cilantro

salt and freshly ground black pepper

For the dressing

¾ cup mayonnaise

2 tbsp Dijon mustard

1 garlic clove, crushed

juice of 1 lime

2 tbsp white wine vinegar

¾ cup freshly grated Parmesan cheese, plus extra Parmesan to shave for garnish

Sun-blush Niçoise

Feeds 6

This is sunshine on a plate—sun-blushed tomatoes, light baby romaine lettuce, olives, and a gorgeous creamy Italian dressing. It's a brilliant appetizer, because it doesn't fill you up too much, but really gets the juices flowing for more tastes. You'll need some foccacia to mop up the irresistible dressing.

1 Break up the lettuces and divide between six bowls or plates.

2 Toss together the potatoes, beans, and capers with a little seasoning, then divide them between the bowls.

3

4 Spoon a little of the dressing over each salad, then sit an egg half, some sun-blushed tomatoes and olives on top or arrange them around the sides of the bowl.

2 baby romaine lettuces

7oz boiled tiny new potatoes (about 12)

7oz cooked fine green beans

5–6 tbsp capers in vinegar

3 hard-cooked eggs, halved

5½oz sun-blushed tomatoes

18 large green olives

salt and freshly ground black pepper

For the Italian dressing—makes 4 cups

4 egg yolks

4 tsp superfine sugar

4 tsp Dijon mustard

2½ cups olive oil

¾ cup white wine vinegar

juice of 3 lemons

freshly chopped oregano leaves

Panzanella

I did some filming in the Tuscany region of Italy a couple of years ago and ended up doing an impromptu cookery demonstration at a wonderful cookery school near Lucca. After I'd finished, about 20 of us sat down and ate some fantastic pasta and fish, but the highlight was the panzanella, which is really just a bell pepper, tomato, and stale bread salad, but using the juice from the tomatoes and the peppery olive oil from the olive groves at the school made it one of my most memorable meals.

1 Skin the tomatoes by putting a cross on the bottom, plunging them into boiling water for about 30 seconds, then into iced water. The skins will peel off easily. Cut them into quarters, scoop out the seeds into a strainer and press to release the juice into a bowl. Put the quarters into a separate bowl.

2 Skin all the peppers by either grilling them, or roasting them until black. Put them in a plastic bag until cool—the skins will fall off. Then seed them and cut each into about eight pieces. Put in the bowl with the tomato quarters, then add the chile, capers, and olives.

3 Tear the bread into big chunks and put in a separate bowl.

4 Add the vinegar, garlic, and oil to the tomato juice, season and whisk well, then pour over the bread and leave for about 1 hour.

5 Finally, gently combine the tomatoes and peppers mixture with the bread and dressing, and garnish with basil leaves.

6 Pretend you're in Tuscany.

2¼lb plum tomatoes

2 red bell peppers

2 yellow bell peppers (you can use green, but they're a little bitter)

1 small red chile, seeded and chopped

5–6 tbsp capers, in vinegar or salt

12 large Ascoloni olives—should be black, but I don't like them so I use green

1 ciabatta loaf, preferably stale

4 tbsp red wine vinegar

5 garlic cloves, crushed

1 cup extra-virgin olive oil, preferably Tuscan

salt and freshly ground black pepper

handful of fresh basil leaves, roughly torn, to garnish

Warm stack of Greek salad with parsley pesto

Feeds 6

A delicious lunch recipe that looks good and yet is simplicity itself. While I say it's Greek, the Italians do help out a bit.

1 Skin the tomatoes by putting a cross on the bottom, plunging them into boiling water for about 30 seconds, then dropping into iced water—the skins will peel off easily. Then slice them to about $\frac{1}{8}$inch thick.

2 Slice the zucchini to the same thickness, season and griddle on both sides until they're nicely striped.

3 To make the pesto, put the garlic and parsley in a blender and whiz together, then with the motor still running add the nuts, cheese, and oil. Taste and season.

4 To assemble, you'll need six 4inch diameter serving rings (or two rings and repeat three times). Sit the rings on a baking sheet. Plonk a layer of tomato in the bottom of each ring. (If you're using plum tomatoes, make sure the base is well covered.) Season, then spoon on a little pesto and top with a couple of basil leaves and a layer of sliced or crumbled feta. Repeat with a layer of zucchini slices. Then repeat the layering, finishing with a layer of feta.

5 Preheat the oven to 350°F. Drizzle the stacks with a little oil and cook in the oven for 10–12 minutes to warm through. You can flash them under a hot broiler to brown, if you want.

6 Unmold each stack onto a plate, and arrange the olives around. Garnish with basil, a good drizzle of oil, and a lemon wedge.

6 beefsteak tomatoes, or
12–15 decent-sized plum tomatoes

1lb zucchini

handful of fresh basil leaves, plus extra for garnish

1lb Greek feta cheese

olive oil for griddling and drizzling

18 large Kalamata black olives

lemon wedges, to serve

salt and freshly ground black pepper

For the parsley pesto

2 garlic cloves

large handful of roughly chopped fresh parsley

$\frac{1}{4}$ cup pine nuts

$\frac{1}{2}$ cup freshly grated Parmesan cheese

$\frac{2}{3}$ cup extra-virgin olive oil, Greek of course

Coronation chickpeas and potato salad

Feeds 8

I used to think coronation chicken was really corny—it probably still is, but I love it. Well, it set me thinking; why didn't Queen Elizabeth get anything created for veggies? So by Royal Appointment, here is something for us.

1 Cook the potatoes and, while they're still hot, cut into quarters and put in a bowl with the onions and vinaigrette. Toss them well (the potatoes will absorb the dressing) and season. Leave to cool.

2 Mix the mayo with the curry paste, then stir into the cooled potatoes with the chickpeas, golden raisins, and almonds. Garnish with cilantro leaves.

800g/1lb 12oz new potatoes, scrubbed

bunch of scallions, finely chopped

2 tbsp vinaigrette

1 cup mayonnaise

2oz smooth curry paste (maybe softened in a little hot water)

½ cup canned chickpeas (garbanzo beans), drained and rinsed

1 tbsp golden raisins

1 tbsp slivered, toasted almonds

salt and freshly ground black pepper

fresh cilantro leaves, to garnish

Asparagus, potato, and fennel salad with Italian dressing

Feeds 4

I love dishes that include a bit of leftover grub—roasties in this case—and teamed with "posh" ingredients such as asparagus. Slap a bit of tangy Italian dressing over the top and it makes a brilliant lunch salad or appetizer.

Slice the asparagus diagonally, cut up the potatoes, if necessary, and put all the salad ingredients into a large bowl. Season well and dress with about ¾ cup of the dressing. (If you like, you can serve this with warm potatoes and asparagus.)

12 cooked asparagus spears

about 20 roast potatoes

2 shallots, sliced

handful of arugula leaves

1 fennel bulb, blanched and finely sliced

1 quantity of Italian dressing (see page 25)

Pickled cucumber salad

Feeds 4

This is dead easy—a lovely sweetish pickle that gives a great lift to any Oriental dish or tired salad. The warm, fragrant Szechuan peppercorns really add to the dish, but if you can't get them use black ones.

1 Toss the cucumber batons in the salt and put in a colander for about 20 minutes to get rid of excess moisture. Meanwhile, dry-fry the peppercorns for 2–3 minutes until fragrant, then roughly grind in a mortar and pestle.

2 Heat the ground nut and chili oils in a small pan, add the garlic and chile and cook gently for 2 minutes. Add the sugar and vinegar and simmer until the sugar has dissolved and the mixture is a little syrupy. Rinse and dry the cucumber and add to the pan with the onions. Crank the heat up and count slowly to 10. Take off the heat, let it cool and serve with whatever you fancy—pie, salad, quiche, Chinese.

4 cucumbers, peeled, seeded, and cut into 2inch long batons

1 tsp salt

2 tbsp Szechuan peppercorns

2 tsp peanut oil

1 tsp chili oil

1 garlic clove, crushed

1 small red chile, seeded and finely chopped

2 tbsp sugar

2 tbsp rice wine vinegar

2 scallions, finely chopped

Sweet potato salad

I do love arugula and Parmesan salad, but arugula deserves more, so I grant it the company of sweet potato and mint.

1 Brush the potato slices with the chili oil and season, then griddle for a couple of minutes on each side.

2 To make the dressing, simply whisk everything together in a small bowl.

3 Put the mint, arugula, and shallots into a serving bowl, pour over the dressing and toss gently, then sit the sweet potatoes on top.

14oz golden sweet potato, peeled and thinly sliced

chili oil

handful of fresh mint leaves

7oz fresh arugula leaves

4 shallots, finely sliced

salt and freshly ground black pepper

For the dressing

1 red chile, seeded and finely chopped

2 tbsp light soy sauce

juice of 1–2 limes

1 tsp superfine sugar

Spicy coleslaw

Feeds 2–4

Wasabi is hot green horseradish—it's seriously fiery, but very addictive.

Put the cabbage, onion, and carrots into a large bowl and season well. Add the mayo, wasabi, and lime leaves and mix it up well.

4oz red cabbage, finely sliced

½ red onion, finely sliced

2 carrots, grated

50g/2oz mayonnaise

¼ cup wasabi paste

3 lime leaves, shredded

salt and freshly ground black pepper

Fattoush

Feeds 4

I think that Middle Eastern cuisine has some of the best veggie dishes and ingredients on the planet—tabbouleh, kibbeh, borak—all great names and tastes (if you don't know what they are, that can be your homework for next time). I also love the fresh, clean tastes they do so well—this brilliant Lebanese salad is ideal for a summer's day, it's crunchy, zesty, and the dressing is divine. Sumac is a dried, crushed berry and it tastes a bit of a cross between cumin and cranberry.

1 To make the dressing, simply whisk all the ingredients together in a bowl.

2 For the salad—again, dead easy—just put all the ingredients in a large bowl and season to taste.

3 Pour the dressing over the salad and gently toss together. I love serving it in a huge bowl and letting everyone pile in.

1 pita bread, torn into small pieces

8 plum tomatoes, seeded and quartered

½ cucumber, peeled, and cut into batons

½ green bell pepper, cut into strips

8 radishes, sliced

1 shallot, sliced

a few arugula leaves

1 small baby romaine lettuce

handful of fresh mint leaves

For the dressing

1¼ cups olive oil

juice and zest of 5 lemons

1 garlic clove, crushed

4 tbsp ground sumac

salt and freshly ground black pepper

Griddled eggplant salad
with nuoc cham

This works brilliantly as a side dish for spicy dishes, but I think it also works as an appetizer. Beware of this Vietnamese dressing, it is HOT, so make use of the yogurt.

1 Put the eggplants into a bowl, add a little oil and the lime juice and season with plenty of salt. Toss well.

2 Next, griddle the eggplants in a hot pan until charred. Put to one side.

3 To make the nuoc cham, simply combine all the ingredients in a processor. (I tend to process the dry ingredients first to make it smooth.)

4 Next, dry-fry the cumin seeds until fragrant, then crush them in a mortar and pestle and combine with the yogurt.

5 Arrange the eggplants on plates, spoon some nuoc cham dressing over, and top with the yogurt.

4 eggplants, cut into wedges,
or chunks if large
vegetable oil for griddling
juice of 1 lime
1 tbsp cumin seeds
½ cup plain yogurt
salt

For the nuoc cham

10 small red chiles
5 garlic cloves
juice of 5 lemons
5 tbsp rice wine vinegar
5 tbsp water

Watermelon salad

This is a great summer dish, making use of juicy watermelon, feta cheese, and the spicy bread. I can feel the sun on my body already.

1 Combine all the ingredients for the dressing in a bowl.

2 Toss the salad ingredients in the dressing, season lightly, then sit some of the salad in a good high mound on top of a piece of coriander seed flat bread (see page 12).

7oz Greek feta cheese, cut into 1inch cubes

½ cucumber, seeded, and cut into 2inch batons

6–8 fresh basil leaves

6 wedges of watermelon, about 3oz each

For the dressing

½ cup Greek yogurt

lots of freshly chopped mint leaves

juice of 1 lime

salt and freshly ground black pepper

Arugula, fig and pecan salad with creamy blue cheese

Feeds 4

This is one of the most delicious ways of eating figs. Traditionally you'd probably expect Roquefort or Dolcelatte, but I'm a champion of trying new tastes, so see what you fancy at your favorite cheese store.

1 Whisk together the oils and vinegar and season well.

2 Put all the remaining ingredients into a large bowl, pour in the dressing, toss together and serve.

2 tbsp walnut oil

1 tbsp vegetable oil

1½ tbsp raspberry vinegar

9oz arugula leaves

½ fennel bulb, very finely sliced

6–8 ripe figs, quartered

5½oz creamy blue cheese, broken into bite-sized cubes

1 cup pecan halves

salt and freshly ground black pepper

Green papaya salad

Feeds 4

I used to eat this hot, spicy salad every day on the beaches on Koh Samui. It's one of those Thai dishes that makes your eyes water and you crave liquid. But take the pain and nibble on raw white cabbage to quell the fire, although ice-cold lager does work well.

1 Put the garlic, shallot, and salt to taste in a large mortar and pestle and grind to a paste. Put the paste in a large serving bowl.

2 Coarsely grate the papaya and add to the bowl with the chiles, tomatoes, beans, nuts, lime juice, and sugar.

3 Garnish with cilantro leaves and lime wedges and serve.

4 garlic cloves

1 shallot, sliced

1 green papaya, peeled and seeded

3 small hot red chiles, seeded and chopped

2 tomatoes, seeded and cut into strips

3 raw green beans, cut into strips

¼ cup roasted peanuts, crushed

juice of 1 lime

pinch of sugar

sea salt

fresh cilantro, to garnish

lime wedges, to serve

Lemon, fennel and oyster mushroom salad

Feeds 4

There's something quite sexy about this salad; maybe it's the lemon marinade combined with the juicy mushrooms and fennel, or maybe it's the way the sauce dribbles down your chin...

1 Trim off the fennel tops, cut the fennel in half lengthwise, or quarters if they're large. Blanch in boiling water for about 1 minute, then plunge into ice-cold water. Drain when cool.

2 Whisk together the oil, lemon juice, zest, and garlic.

3 Arrange the mushrooms and fennel in a serving dish and season well, then pour over the oil marinade. Add enough oil to just cover the ingredients. Cover and chill for at least 24 hours, then serve with warm foccacia bread to dip into the sauce.

3 fennel bulbs

lots of extra-virgin olive oil

juice and zest of 3 lemons

2 garlic cloves, sliced

7oz oyster mushrooms

salt and freshly ground black pepper

Small platefuls

Eggplant "roll-mops"

Feeds 4

I love roll-mop herrings, they remind me of my dad, as we're the only members of my family who like them. I created this eggplant version almost as a joke, but I found that everyone loved them, so now you can make them. You really need to pickle the onions for at least a week, otherwise you'll be pulling faces as you eat. If you want to make this more substantial serve with cold boiled potatoes, hard-cooked eggs, and fine green beans.

1 To pickle the onions, put all the ingredients except the onions in a pan and bring to a slow boil. Simmer for 15 minutes, then allow to cool. Pack the onions into a sterilized sealable jar and pour the spiced vinegar over them. Seal the jar and leave for at least 1 week.

2 To assemble the dish, cut the eggplants into strips about ⅛inch thick. Season the strips, then brush with the oil and cook on a griddle for a minute or so each side until nicely striped.

3 Put a little bit of pickled onion (make sure you don't have any seeds in there) at the end of a slice of eggplant, roll it up tightly and secure with a wooden toothpick. When you've rolled them all up pour a little more vinegar over and chill for about 20 minutes.

4 Make a dressing by whisking the chopped chives into the cream.

5 Sit a couple of roll-mops on a little watercress or other greenery and top with a big dollop of the chive cream.

3 large eggplants, topped and tailed
olive oil for brushing
white vinegar for drizzling
freshly chopped chives
¾ cup sour cream
salt and freshly ground black pepper
watercress, to serve (optional)

For the pickled onions

4 cups white vinegar
1 cinnamon stick
6 cloves
1 tbsp coriander seeds
1 tsp mustard seeds
2 bay leaves
2 red chiles
1 tsp black peppercorns
2 tbsp superfine sugar
1½ tbsp salt
2 onions, finely sliced

Eggplant tikka

This might seem like a bit of a hassle for lunch, but it is worth it and even though there are a lot of ingredients it's easy to prepare. The end result is fantastic, ideal for outdoor summery lunches with friends.

1 Toss the eggplants in oil and salt, then cook on a hot griddle pan on each side until striped.

2 Put all the marinade ingredients into a large bowl and stir to mix. Coat the eggplants well with the marinade, thread onto wooden skewers and put into a dish, then cover and chill for at least 2 hours.

3 To make the coleslaw, simply combine all the ingredients in a bowl.

4 Cook the eggplants under a hot broiler, basting with the butter and lemon juice and turning when golden.

5 Serve the eggplant kebabs with a few chiles, lime wedges, and the coleslaw.

4–6 eggplants, about 2lb, topped, tailed and cut into chunks

vegetable oil

3½ tbsp melted butter

juice of 1 lemon

salt

chiles and lime wedges, to serve

For the marinade

½ cup plain yogurt

juice of 1 lime

2 garlic cloves, crushed

1inch piece of fresh ginger, finely chopped

1 tbsp ground coriander

1 tsp ground cumin

1 tsp garam masala

1 tsp paprika

For the coleslaw

1 cup plain yogurt

juice of 2 limes

pinch of cayenne pepper

6oz shredded white cabbage

1 each of red, yellow and orange bell peppers

10 scallions, chopped

handful of freshly chopped cilantro leaves and stems

1 tbsp ground cumin

1 garlic clove, crushed

Eggplant "stack" with pesto

Feeds 4

Imagine yourself in Italy—Florence with the beauty of the city, the fine ice cream and brilliant small restaurants knocking out exquisite Italian fare—then imagine a local guy has opened a sandwich bar using all these influences, that's what this is all about.

1 Preheat the oven to 400°F. To make the pesto, put the basil and a little of the oil in a food processor and blitz to make a paste. Add the garlic, pine nuts and Parmesan and blitz with enough oil to make a rich, thick sauce. Turn out into a dish, check the seasoning and keep the pesto cool.

2 Season the eggplants well and toss in oil, then cook on a hot griddle pan on both sides until striped. Do the same with the bread.

3 To assemble the dish, put four rings (about 4inches wide x 2inches deep) on a baking sheet and brush a little oil around the inside of each.

4 Press some eggplant into the bottom to form a solid base, then add a slice of tomato and a spoonful of pesto. Then it's a piece of bread, a little oil and mozzarella. Continue layering and finish with a layer of cheese. Drizzle with oil, then cook in the oven for 10–15 minutes until warmed through. Finish off under a hot broiler to brown the cheese before serving.

5 Sit each ring on a plate, run a knife around the inside edge and carefully remove the ring. Garnish with a little dressed arugula.

3–4 good-sized eggplants, topped, tailed and sliced into ½inch rounds

vegetable oil for griddling and brushing

1 ciabatta, cut into slices about the thickness of a dollar coin

9oz beefsteak tomatoes, thinly sliced

10oz buffalo mozzarella cheese, thinly sliced

dressed arugula leaves, to garnish

For the pesto

10oz fresh basil, stalks and leaves

½ cup extra-virgin olive oil

2 garlic cloves

½ cup toasted pine nuts

1 cup freshly grated Parmesan cheese

salt and freshly ground black pepper

Goat's cheese and mango

Feeds 6

Another Greens classic and probably one of the easiest dishes ever created, it's cheese on toast for goodness sake. This has been on and off the menu for thirteen years and there's still an argument raging as to who actually created it. The dish was conceived around a table at a curry house after a good few beers. Now we all claim to be the daddy of the dish, but I think we know the truth...

1 Preheat the oven to 250ºF. Dip a sharp knife into really hot water, then slice the cheese log into pieces about ⅓inch thick (this will give about six portions). Dip the knife into the water after each slice.

2 Combine the sesame seeds, chile and mint in a wide bowl.

3 Warm the honey, then brush it sparingly on one side of each piece of cheese. Press the cheese slices into the sesame mixture then shake off any excess. Put to one side.

4 Cut a circle a little bigger than a cheese slice out of each piece of bread (probably a 3inch cutter). Brush each bread slice with a little oil, then put in the oven for about 5 minutes until dry, but not colored.

5 To make the sauce, put the wine, mango, and salt into a bowl and mix well.

6 When you're ready to serve, put a piece of cheese on each slice of bread and either put under a hot broiler until the cheese softens, but not melts, or put it in a hottish oven (400ºF) for a few minutes.

7 Put a swirl or small pool of sauce in the middle of each plate, top with a little arugula, then sit the cheese on toast on top.

7oz goat's cheese log, rind on

1¼ cups toasted sesame seeds

2 small red chiles, finely chopped

1 bunch of fresh mint leaves, finely chopped

5 tbsp clear honey

6 thick slices white loaf

olive oil

splash of white wine

7fl oz canned mango pulp

pinch of salt

arugula leaves, to serve

Mushroom "rarebit" on brioche toast

Feeds 6

I love the taste and texture of field mushrooms and when you add the strong cheesy topping and serve it on toasted brioche, well, it's the food of kings and queens.

1 Preheat the oven to 350°F. Put the mushrooms in a baking dish and season. Sprinkle with garlic and cover with the oil. Cook in the oven for 10–12 minutes until softened slightly.

2 Meanwhile, toast the brioche and make the rarebit topping by combining all the ingredients in a bowl. When the mushrooms come out of the oven spoon some of the topping mix onto each of them, pressing it well in. Then place under a hot broiler until the cheese bubbles, melts and browns.

3 Serve one large mushroom on top of a piece of toasted brioche.

6 large field mushrooms, or portobellos cut in half, peeled and trimmed

2 garlic cloves, crushed

½ cup olive oil

6 slices brioche

salt and freshly ground black pepper

For the topping

2 cups grated mature Cheddar or Gruyère cheese

1 tbsp wholegrain mustard

1 garlic clove, crushed

1 egg, beaten

Proper pizza

Pizzas originated in Naples as a way of using up leftovers, such as bread dough, tomatoes, cheese, and herbs. Since then, of course, they've become a bit of a hybrid—asparagus and fontina, Sunday lunch pizza, even balti pizza. Well this is a simple, but delicious, Neapolitan pizza with tomatoes, cheese, basil, and olive oil. Once you've mastered this, then if you want to try apricot and radish tikka masala pizza, well who am I to criticize?

1 To make the base, sift the flour into a large bowl. Dissolve the yeast in a little warm water until it begins to foam, then slowly add to the flour and mix to form a dough. If it's too sticky add more flour.

2 Cover the bowl and leave to rest for 5 minutes. Turn out onto a lightly floured surface and knead the dough with the salt for about 10 minutes until smooth. Cover with a damp cloth and let it prove for about 30 minutes.

3 Preheat the oven to 475°F. Cut the dough in half, knead for a brief minute, then press it out into two circles about 1½inches diameter each (I like the edges slightly thicker, almost like a plate edge). Place the dough circles on floured baking sheets.

4 To make the topping, season the tomatoes and spread over each dough base (you probably won't need the whole can). Add some basil leaves, seasoning, and torn cheese to each one, then drizzle over some oil.

5 Put in the oven and bake for 8–10 minutes.

6 Serve with a little more oil and some black pepper.

*If using dried yeast, follow the maker's instructions for quantity and use.

For the base

4½ cups bread flour, plus extra for dusting

10g/¼oz fresh yeast*

2 tsp salt

For the topping

15oz can chopped tomatoes, well drained

fresh basil leaves

7oz buffalo mozzarella cheese, torn into pieces

extra-virgin olive oil

salt and freshly ground black pepper

Pumpkin enchilladas
with mole sauce

Feeds 6

I adore Mexican food—it can be a bit limited, but what's good is magnificent, like this dish. Mole sauce is a rich, deep, smoky sauce with both a chocolate and chile hit. I leave the seeds in the chiles, but take them out if you prefer. I like to serve this with guacamole and sour cream. Don't turn the page thinking this weird choccy sauce isn't for you—it is! Try it and be converted.

1 To make the sauce, put the chiles, coriander seeds, sesame seeds, almonds, peppercorns, and cloves in a mortar and pestle and crush. Tip into a skillet and dry-fry for a minute or so until lightly charred.

2 In a separate pan, fry the onion, garlic, and cocoa in a little oil for 2 minutes.

3 Add the tomatoes and bring to a boil, then add all the dry-fried spices, the cinnamon, sugar, and stock and cook for 25 minutes. Transfer to a blender and whiz until smooth. Turn out and fold in the chocolate.

4 Preheat the oven to 400°F. Put some oil in a roasting pan and put in the oven to heat up. Tip the squash into the roasting pan, season well and roast for 40 minutes until soft.

5 Put the squash in a bowl, add the refried beans, cilantro, and red chile and stir well to mix.

6 Divide the mixture between the tortillas, roll up and cut the ends straight. Put in a baking dish, cover, and cook in the oven for about 12 minutes, until warmed through.

7 To serve, put two tortillas on each plate and spoon over some of the sauce (it's pretty heady so not too much). Serve with some sour cream, lime wedges, and cilantro.

vegetable oil for roasting

2 butternut squash, peeled and cut into 1¼inch cubes

15oz can refried beans

freshly chopped cilantro leaves

1 red chile, chopped

12 soft flour or corn tortillas

salt and freshly ground black pepper

soured cream, lime wedges and fresh cilantro leaves, to serve

For the sauce

10 red chiles

2 tsp coriander seeds

1 tsp sesame seeds

2 tbsp slivered almonds

5 black peppercorns

2–3 cloves

1 onion, sliced

3 garlic cloves, crushed

1 tbsp cocoa powder

vegetable oil for frying

15oz can chopped tomatoes

pinch of cinnamon

sugar to taste

⅔ cup stock

3½oz best-quality dark chocolate (not unsweetened), grated

Chinese mushroom pancakes

Creating vegan dishes is always really difficult, so when I made this for the first time I thought I was the vegan king! It takes its inspiration from crispy duck and pancakes, but we're using oyster mushrooms instead—it really is brilliant.

1 To make the sauce, heat a little oil in a skillet and fry the shallots until soft.

2 Add the garlic and sherry, reduce a little, then add the plums and cook until they begin to break down. Add the stock and bring to a boil.

3 Simmer for 5 minutes, then pass through a strainer into a serving bowl.

4 Mix the flour and five-spice powder together with some seasoning. Toss the mushrooms in the mix, then shake off any excess.

5 Heat some oil in a large pan and deep-fry the mushrooms in batches for about 4 minutes, until crisp and brown. Drain well on paper towels.

6 Warm the pancakes either in a microwave for 20 seconds or in a steamer over simmering water for 1 minute.

7 I like to pile the mushrooms onto one big plate, put the cucumber and scallions on another and the pancakes inside the steamer. Spread a little plum sauce on a pancake, lay a strip of mushrooms down the middle, top with onion and cucumber, and roll up, tucking in the bottom edge. Guzzle down and make sure you've got extra pancakes on hand, because everyone will want more.

$7/8$ cup all-purpose flour

$7/8$ cup five-spice powder

14oz oyster mushrooms

18 Chinese pancakes, 3inch diameter (from any Asian supermarkets)

1 cucumber, seeded and cut into 2inch batons

6–8 scallions, finely sliced

vegetable oil for deep-frying

salt and freshly ground black pepper

For the plum sauce

2 shallots, chopped

1 garlic clove, crushed

splash of dry sherry

1lb plums, pitted

$1/2$ cup stock

vegetable oil

Banana dhal

You can use any type of lentil to make a dhal, but the advantage of the red ones is that they don't have to be soaked, so this makes a really quick and easy meal. Adding either fresh banana or fried plantain makes it extra special and all you need to serve with it are a couple of chapattis.

1 Fry the onion, garlic, and ginger, in the oil over a low heat for about 10 minutes until soft and golden. Add the turmeric and cook for 1 minute.

2 Add the lentils to the pan and fry for 1–2 minutes.

3 Add the warmed stock and bring to a boil, then simmer for 15 minutes.

4 Add the spices, season, and cook for a further 10 minutes.

5 A couple of minutes before serving fold in the bananas and warm through.

6 Garnish with cilantro leaves and eat with bread.

1 onion, finely sliced

2 garlic cloves, chopped

1inch piece of fresh ginger, finely chopped

2 tbsp vegetable oil

pinch of turmeric

1 generous cup red lentils, well washed and drained

3 cups warmed stock

pinch of ground cumin

pinch of ground coriander

pinch of garam masala

4 firm bananas, thinly sliced

salt and freshly ground black pepper

fresh cilantro leaves, to garnish

Gruyère-filled beefsteak tomatoes

Feeds 4

This is a really old dish from Greens, but I still love it. The intense flavor from reducing the cream, then adding yummy Gruyère cheese and tasty treats makes it what I like to call a meat-eater's veggie dish.

1 Preheat the oven to 325°F. Skin the tomatoes by putting a cross on the bottom, plunging them into boiling water for about 30 seconds, then into iced water. The skins will peel off easily. Slice off the tops and put to one side, scoop out the pulp into a bowl, being careful not to break the flesh, and put the pulp to one side. Season the cavities well.

2 Put the cream in a heavy-bottom pan, bring slowly up to a boil, then cook to reduce the volume by half.

3 Meanwhile, heat a little oil in a large pan and gently fry the zucchini, peppers, mushrooms, and garlic until soft, about 5 minutes.

4 Add $2/3$ cup of the cheese to the reduced cream and stir until it melts. Remove from the heat and fold in the fried vegetables.

5 Divide the filling between the tomatoes, top with the remaining cheese, sit the lids on top and put onto a baking sheet.

6 Cook in the oven for 6–8 minutes, until the cheese melts.

7 To make the dressing, press the tomato pulp through a strainer and season the juices. Add the vinegar, then whisk in the oil.

8 Toss the arugula in the dressing and sit the tomatoes on top of the leaves.

4 beefsteak tomatoes

1¾ cups heavy cream

2 zucchini, finely diced

2 red bell peppers, seeded and finely diced

3oz white button mushrooms, finely chopped

1 garlic clove, crushed

1¾ cups freshly grated Gruyère cheese

vegetable oil for frying

salt and freshly ground black pepper

handful of fresh arugula leaves, to serve

For the dressing

tomato pulp from the tomatoes

1½ tbsp red wine vinegar

5 tbsp extra-virgin olive oil

Roasted red bell peppers with fennel

Feeds 6

Patience is the key for this recipe, the peppers and fennel need to be soft, and the cheese needs to brown and bubble—if you rush this it'll be a big disappointment.

1 Preheat the oven to 400°F. Season the peppers well, drizzle with oil, then put in a baking pan and roast for about 10 minutes until softened.

2 Blanch the fennel pieces in boiling salted water for 2 minutes, then plunge into ice-cold water. When they're cool, pat dry.

3 Put the tomatoes and olives in a bowl with the garlic and parsley and season well.

4 Put a piece of fennel inside each pepper half, sprinkle some tomato mixture over and drizzle with oil. Top with grated cheese and put under a hot broiler until the cheese bubbles and browns.

5 To serve, put a little watercress on each plate and sit a pepper half on top. Spoon some yogurt on the side and garnish with a lemon wedge and green olives. Finish with a good twist of black pepper.

3 decent-sized red bell peppers, halved lengthwise and seeded

3 fennel bulbs, trimmed and cut into halves, or quarters if very large

3 tomatoes, skinned, seeded, and finely chopped

3–4 black olives, pitted and finely chopped

1 garlic clove, crushed

small handful of freshly chopped parsley

10oz mozzarella cheese, grated

olive oil for roasting

salt and freshly ground black pepper

watercress or mesclun, Greek yogurt, lemon wedges and green olives, to serve

Peas
and carrots

Make this and don't tell your friends and family what's in it, they'll struggle to guess. Mint, peas, carrot vinaigrette—such simple ingredients, but combined they're pretty cool, and very much removed from the frozen or tinned stuff. It makes a great appetizer.

1 Preheat the oven to 350°F. Blanch the peas in boiling salted water for 1 minute, then plunge into ice-cold water. Drain well, then purée with the mint in a food processor.

2 Combine the eggs, cream, and lemon juice in a bowl and season to taste. Pass the pea purée through a fine strainer into the egg mixture.

3 Divide the mixture between six greased ramekins. Put them in a roasting pan, pour in hot water to about half way up the ramekins, cover with foil and cook in the oven for 25–30 minutes until set. Allow to cool.

4 To make the dressing, put ¾ cup of the carrot juice into a pan, bring to the boil, reduce the heat and cook until reduced by half. Pour into a bowl, add the honey and vinegar and whisk to mix. Slowly add the oil, then stir in the rest of the carrot juice and season.

5 Turn out each pea custard onto a plate. Toss some chard in the dressing, sit this on top of the pea creation and drizzle more dressing around.

3 cups defrosted frozen peas (fresh if in season)

lots of fresh mint leaves

3 eggs

¾ cup heavy cream

squeeze of lemon juice

salt and freshly ground black pepper

red chard, to garnish

For the dressing

1 cup carrot juice (squeeze your own if you can)

1 tsp honey

1 tbsp white wine vinegar

⅔ cup extra-virgin olive oil

Leeks wrapped in phyllo

This is a simple and delicious starter packed with flavor. Avoid using really huge leeks as they're a bit "woody" for this dish; what you need are slim, attractive leeks that will be sweet and succulent.

1 Preheat the oven to 425ºF. Cut the leeks into 4inch long pieces (cut the end at an angle to make them look pretty).

2 Heat some oil in a roasting pan, then put all the leeks in, season well and add the garlic. Roast in the oven for about 5 minutes until just a little soft. Take out of the oven and cool, then peel off their outer layer.

3 When the leeks are cool, cut the phyllo to the length of the leeks and wrap a piece around each leek. Brush with butter, put in the roasting pan and pop back in the oven for another 8–10 minutes until the phyllo is crisp and golden.

4 To make the dressing, whisk the lemon juice and mustard together, then add the garlic and whisk in the oil. Fold in the chives and tomatoes and season well.

5 Sit a little watercress or other greenery on each plate, top with two leek parcels and spoon over a little dressing.

6 medium-sized leeks, trimmed, well washed and dried

1 garlic clove, sliced

6 sheets of phyllo pastry

3oz melted butter

olive oil for roasting

salt and freshly ground black pepper

a little watercress, to serve (optional)

For the dressing

juice of 2 lemons

3oz Dijon (Grey Poupon) mustard

1 garlic clove, crushed

⅔ cup extra-virgin olive oil

handful of freshly chopped chives

2oz sun-blushed tomatoes, finely chopped

Leek and potato rosti with "rarebit" topping

Feeds 6

Rostis are simply fried grated potato with added bits—leeks in this case—and yummy toppings. They're easy to do: simply grate the potatoes, mold into a disc and fry—but sometimes those pesky potatoes don't want to stick together and you end up with burnt potato pieces, not nice. So this is a fail-safe way to perfect rosti every time, by par-boiling the potatoes they'll stick like glue, and it means you can prepare them in advance without worrying about them.

1 Put the potatoes in a pan and just cover with water, bring to a boil and then boil for 7 minutes, no more. Drain.

2 When they're cool enough to handle, peel the potatoes and grate them into a bowl. If you use long strokes the end result is better, or you can use the grater attachment on your processor.

3 Mix the grated potatoes with the leek and garlic, then season really well.

4 Mold the mixture into six patties and chill for 1 hour.

5 Heat a good amount of oil in a pan, enough so when you put the rosti in it will lap up the side a little. Pop in the rostis (do in two batches) and fry over medium heat for about 4 minutes each side until golden, then drain on paper towels.

6 To make the topping, put the ingredients into a bowl and stir well to mix.

7 Lay out all the rostis on a baking sheet and divide the topping between them, then place under a hot broiler until the cheese bubbles and browns.

8 This is delicious served with tomato and balsamic vinegar salad, or a fried egg—honestly!

4 large potatoes, scrubbed but not peeled

1 small leek, trimmed, well washed and finely chopped

2 garlic cloves, crushed

vegetable oil for frying

lots of salt and freshly ground black pepper

For the topping

2½ cups freshly grated strong mature Cheddar cheese

1 egg, beaten

1½ tbsp wholegrain mustard

Beet tart

I love this and the combination of buttery pastry, sweet roasted beets and sharp tangy goat's cheese is delicious.

1 To make the pastry, put the butter, flour and salt in a food processor and pulse until it resembles breadcrumbs. Add the water and milk and pulse to form a dough. Turn into a bowl, cover and chill for 25 minutes.

2 Preheat the oven to 400°F. Divide the pastry into four and roll out to roughly fit deep tart pans, about 4–4½ inches wide. Line the pans, letting the pastry overhang the edges a little, and bake blind for 25–30 minutes until firm and lightly golden. Remove from the oven and trim off the edges.

3 To make the chutney, fry the onions, garlic, and butter with some seasoning in a little oil over a low heat for about 20 minutes until golden but not burnt. Add the sugar and vinegar, bring to a boil, then reduce the heat right the way down and cook for about 30 minutes until "jammy".

4 To make the filling, chuck the broccoli into boiling salted water, count to 10, then spoon it out and plunge into iced water (this will stop it cooking on). Drain well.

5 Heat some oil in a skillet, then add the beets, season well and cook for a couple of minutes. Add the broccoli and pine nuts (these are yummy if you toast them a little first) and cook for a minute or two. Pour in the crushed tomatoes and toss all the ingredients quickly, then remove from the heat.

6 Divide the filling mixture between the pans and top with the crumbled goat's cheese. Either flash under a hot broiler until the cheese browns, or put back into the top of the oven for a few minutes.

7 Serve alongside the chutney. This is really fab with big fat fries with rock salt and balsamic vinegar.

For the pastry

1¾ sticks chilled butter, cut into cubes

3¼ cups all-purpose flour

pinch of salt

3½ tbsp water

3½ tbsp milk

For the filling

12 broccoli florets

4–6 cooked beets, peeled and cut into large wedges

¾ cup pine nuts

½ cup crushed tomatoes

6oz goat's cheese, crumbled

vegetable oil for frying

salt and freshly ground black pepper

For the chutney

4 large Spanish onions, sliced

1 garlic clove, crushed

½ stick butter

⅔ cup dark brown sugar

½ cup white wine vinegar

vegetable oil for frying

salt and freshly ground black pepper

Simple
tomato tart

Every time I make this I forget how easy it is and yet it looks like you've taken ages to make it. Serve with some arugula dressed with extra-virgin olive oil and balsamic vinegar.

1 Preheat the oven to 350ºF. Roll out the pastry on a lightly floured surface to an 7 x 11inch rectangle and put on a greased baking sheet.

2 Cut the tomatoes into slices about $\frac{1}{8}$inch thick. Arrange overlapping slices on the pastry, leaving a 1inch border all round. Season well, brush with butter and sprinkle with sugar.

3 Bake in the oven for 25–30 minutes, until crisp and golden and the tomatoes have caramelized.

4 Combine the oil and vinegar in a bowl and toss the arugula in it. Serve a generous slice of tart on each plate with the dressed arugula.

8oz bought puff pastry

flour for dusting

6–8 plum tomatoes, peeled

2 tbsp melted butter, plus extra for greasing

1 tbsp superfine sugar

3 tbsp extra-virgin olive oil

1 tbsp balsamic vinegar

fresh arugula leaves

salt and freshly ground black pepper

Sun-dried tomato, mozzarella and basil tart

Feeds 6

This is so simple and yet so tasty. If you ever make a cheese-filled tart, always add a little splash of cream to give a touch of richness to the filling. All you need with this is a bit of green salad dressed with simple vinaigrette.

1 Divide the pastry into six equal pieces and roll out on a lightly floured surface to fit six 4inch tart pans. Press the pastry into the pans, then chill them for about 20 minutes.

2 Preheat the oven to 400°F. Put the pans on a baking sheet and bake for 15 minutes until crisp and golden.

3 To make the filling, combine the cheese, basil, and tomatoes in a large bowl and season well.

4 When the pans are cooked, remove from the oven, divide the filling between them and add a splash of cream to each. Return to the oven and bake for about 5 minutes until the cheese melts and begins to brown.

1 quantity of shortcrust pastry (see page 92)

flour for dusting

2½ cups freshly grated mozzarella cheese

about 20 fresh basil leaves

12 sun-dried tomatoes, finely chopped

dash of heavy cream

salt and freshly ground black pepper

Spicy beet and
coconut soup

Feeds 6

Beets get a lot of bad press and everybody, except me, seems to hate pickled beet. I love it and it also has magical properties. Whenever I go to watch an important soccer match with my mates, it's tradition for me to bring the lucky cheese and beet sandwiches—they nearly always work. Anyway, this is one of the most stunning and delicious soups you'll ever make, it's both earthy and spicy at the same time and it has the best color pink. A little tip: don't blend it until you're about to serve as it will go brownish.

1 Put all the ingredients for the paste into a blender and blend until smooth (the smoother the paste the nicer the soup, so take your time).

2 Preheat the oven to 400°F. Put the scrubbed beets into an ovenproof dish, sprinkle with oil and sea salt, then wrap in foil and roast for about 35 minutes until soft. When cool enough to handle, peel and chop the beets.

3 Gently fry the shallots and cumin seeds in a little oil, then add half the paste and cook for 5 minutes to release the fragrance.

4 Add half the beets, cook for a couple of minutes, then add the stock, bring to a boil and simmer for about 7–8 minutes.

5 This is when it gets interesting—just before serving, put the soup, coconut milk, the rest of the paste and beets in a blender and blend until smooth. It will be a bright pink, like you've never seen from food before, unless you live on Mars. The soup should be hot enough, but if necesssary reheat gently for a minute or two.

6 Check the seasoning, then serve immediately topped with mint, cilantro and cucumber. It's also lovely with the coriander seed flat bread (see page 12).

1lb 2oz fresh beets, scrubbed
vegetable oil for coating and frying
2 banana shallots, finely chopped
1 tsp cumin seeds
2½ cups stock
1¾ cups coconut milk
sea salt
fresh mint, cilantro leaves and chopped, seeded cucumber, to serve

For the paste

2 stalks of lemon grass
2 garlic cloves
3 red chiles (seeded if you like)
1inch piece of fresh ginger, peeled
4 kaffir lime leaves
juice of 1 lime

Big platefuls

Huevos rancheros (ranch eggs)

Feeds 4

A good few years ago my dear friend Graham Peers got married in Richmond, Virginia, so a tribe of us made the trip and we all stayed at various friends of Graham's around town. Alison, my wife, and I got the best deal as we were 50 yards from a fantastic place called The Steak and Eggs Kitchen, which did the best breakfasts, and had those mini-TVs on the tables. Well, this is where I first had huevos rancheros, or fried eggs cooked with spicy salsa and flour tortillas on the side. Serve these with extra-hot chili sauce and endless cups of coffee.

1 Put all the ingredients for the salsa except the crushed tomatoes in a bowl and season. Gradually add the crushed tomatoes—you may find you don't need them all, you're looking for the veg bits to be bound by the tomato sauce, not swimming in it.

2 You need to cook this in batches. Heat a little oil in a skillet over a medium heat and warm a quarter of the salsa. Now make a hole in the middle of the pan, melt a ½ stick butter in the gap, then break 2 eggs into this space. Put a lid on the pan and leave for about 3 minutes. The dish is ready when the eggs are cooked and the whites have merged into the salsa.

3 Slide the eggs and salsa onto a large plate and top with cilantro leaves. Cook the rest of the eggs in the same way. Now dip your warm tortillas into the yolks and dare yourself to overdo the chili sauce. (Not that I'd know, but apparently this is a great hangover cure!)

vegetable oil for frying

2 sticks (1 cup) butter

8 eggs

fresh cilantro leaves

2 warm soft flour or corn tortillas, halved

hot chili sauce (Jamaican hot is pretty good)

For the salsa

1 onion, finely chopped

1 red bell pepper, seeded and finely chopped

1 small hot red chile, finely chopped

1 zucchini, finely chopped

1 garlic clove, finely chopped

1 green bell pepper, seeded and finely chopped

⅔ cup crushed tomatoes

salt and freshly ground black pepper

Savory Paris-Brest

This is traditionally a sweet dish with custard, almonds, and other yummy things inside a ring of choux pastry. I don't see any reason why you can't turn it on its head and have a savory filling—so I will.

1 Preheat the oven to 400ºF. To make the pastry, put the butter and water in a pan and heat until the butter melts, then bring to a boil. Take the pan off the heat, tip in all the flour and mix well. Cool slightly, then, using a wooden spoon, beat in the eggs, one at a time (it's pretty tough on the old arms, this one). Add the salt.

2 Transfer to a pastry bag and allow to cool for a few minutes. Line a baking sheet with waxed paper, then pipe a 8inch diameter circle onto the paper, then pipe another one directly on top.

3 Put the sheet in the oven and cook for 30–40 minutes, when the choux ring should be golden and firm. The aim is to get it to dry out in the middle—I quite often put it on the bottom shelf for another 5–10 minutes to make sure. When it's cooked, take the ring out and let it cool. Increase the oven temperature to 425ºF.

4 To make the filling, heat some oil on a baking sheet in the oven. Slice the zucchini and eggplant into pieces about $\frac{1}{8}$inch thick. Ideally, cook each vegetable separately—season each vegetable, place in the hot oil on the sheet, add a little garlic and roast until soft, then toss in a little thyme. Put to one side while you cook the next one. However, if you're pushed for time, roast the onions for 5 minutes, then add the peppers for 5 minutes, then the eggplant and zucchini in the same sheet.

5 When all the vegetables are roasted, reduce the oven temperature to 350ºF. Slice the choux ring horizontally into two halves. Arrange the vegetables on the bottom ring and top with the sun-blushed tomatoes and goat's cheese. Cover with the top ring.

6 Pop it back into the oven for about 10 minutes until the cheese softens. Serve with a dressed mixed leaf salad.

$1\frac{1}{4}$ sticks butter (10 tbsp)
1 cup water
$1\frac{3}{4}$ cups all-purpose flour
6 eggs
pinch of salt

For the filling

2 zucchini
1 eggplant
1 red onion, sliced in quarters attached to the base
2 red bell peppers, seeded and cut into chunks
1 garlic clove
fresh thyme
12 sun-blushed tomatoes
7oz goat's cheese, crumbled
vegetable oil for roasting
salt and freshly ground black pepper

Phyllo strudel with port wine sauce   Feeds 6

OK, here we go, the recipe that changed the world, well Greens. I always say this is the dish to serve to meat-eaters because it blows their minds. I like to serve it with some fine green beans with garlic and tomato sauce (see page 106) and a few new potatoes, although a good friend of mine swears it tastes best with fries and garlic mayo. If you make only one dish out of this book, it should be this one…

1 Heat some oil in a pan, add the mushrooms, garlic, and seasoning and fry for a couple of minutes, then drain well. Then fry the leeks.

2 Mix the cheeses together in a large bowl with a good amount of seasoning until smooth. (Sometimes it helps to warm the cream cheese for a few seconds in a microwave to soften it.) Fold in the mushrooms, leeks, and tomatoes, then chill for at least 2 hours.

3 Preheat the oven to 400°F. Lay out six pieces of pastry on a lightly floured surface and brush with lots of melted butter, then cover with another layer and brush again. Add a final layer, but this time only brush the edges of the pastry.

4 Divide the chilled filling into six long sausages and place each one on the bottom edge of each pastry rectangle. Fold the bottom edge over the filling, tuck in the sides, then roll up into a tight parcel and brush with butter. Put them all on a baking sheet and cook in the oven for 25 minutes until crisp and golden.

5 Meanwhile, make the sauce. Pour the wine into a pan, bring to a boil and reduce it by half—stick a bay leaf in the wine if you want to make it a little more "herby."

6 Heat the oil in a pan and cook the onion, mushrooms, and garlic with seasoning until soft. Throw in a big slosh of port and reduce that by half. Next, pour in the reduced wine and bring back to a boil, then add the stock, bring to a boil and cook to reduce for about 15 minutes. Just before serving, whisk in the cold butter to give it a really great shine.

7 To serve, pour a little sauce on each plate and sit a strudel on top.

7oz button mushrooms, halved

1 garlic clove, crushed

7oz leeks, trimmed, well washed, drained and roughly chopped

9oz ricotta cheese

9oz full-fat cream cheese

3 tomatoes, skinned, seeded and chopped

18 pieces phyllo pastry, 9 x 6inch melted butter

olive oil for frying

salt and freshly ground black pepper

For the sauce

1 bottle red wine (a good heavy red is best)

1 bay leaf (optional)

2 tbsp olive oil

1 large onion, sliced

3oz button mushrooms, sliced

2 garlic cloves, crushed

good glug of port

½ cup stock

¼ stick (2 tbsp) cold butter, cubed

Wild mushroom pancakes

Feeds 6

The filling for these pancakes is rich and delicious and the pecans make it a brilliant dish for the winter. Unlike in most pancake recipes, you don't need to let the batter stand.

1 First make the pancakes. Sift the flour and salt into a bowl, then make a well in the center and break the eggs into it. Whisk the eggs into the flour, then, little by little, slowly add the milk and water, whisking well to avoid lumps. Finally, whisk in the butter.

2 Heat a little oil in an 7inch skillet until really hot, then turn the heat down to medium. Spoon about 4 tbsp of batter into the pan and swirl it around to evenly coat the base. Cook the pancake for about 30 seconds, then flip it over and cook the other side. Turn the pancake out onto greaseproof paper and repeat with the rest of the batter. You should get twelve pancakes. Stack each pancake on waxed paper until you're ready to use them.

3 For the filling, mix the ricotta and Parmesan cheeses together and season well.

4 Heat a little oil in a pan and fry the fresh shiitakes and garlic for about 5 minutes, then drain on paper towels. Drain off the water from the dried mushrooms and chop them up.

5 Combine all the mushrooms, the pecans, and tarragon with the cheese mixture and check the seasoning.

6 Preheat the oven to 350°F. Put about 4 tbsp of filling across each pancake and roll up, tucking in the ends to make a neat parcel.

7 Use two pancakes per serving. Put the pancakes on a greased baking sheet or in pairs in greased individual dishes and top each pair with grated mozzarella. Cook in the oven for about 15 minutes until the cheese melts. Serve with a little ladleful of warm tomato sauce and some fine green beans with garlic and tomato sauce (see page 106).

$\frac{7}{8}$ cup all-purpose flour

pinch of salt

2 eggs

$\frac{3}{4}$ cup milk

$\frac{1}{2}$ cup water

$\frac{1}{2}$ stick (4 tbsp) butter, melted

1$\frac{3}{4}$ cups freshly grated mozzarella cheese

vegetable oil for frying

$\frac{1}{2}$ quantity basic tomato sauce (see page 107), to serve

For the filling

1lb ricotta cheese

1$\frac{1}{2}$ cups freshly grated Parmesan cheese

6oz fresh shiitake mushrooms

1 garlic clove, crushed

3oz dried shiitake mushrooms, soaked in boiling water for 1 hour

1 cup slightly broken pecans

2oz freshly chopped tarragon leaves

salt and freshly ground black pepper

Hazelnut and mushroom parcels

Feeds 4

This is another "meaty" dish that any carnivores will adore. Mushrooms, hazelnuts, and cheese wrapped in puff pastry—how could that not be anything but gorgeous? Great for Sunday lunch, or even Christmas, maybe with some fresh cranberries inside and a Cumberland sauce, but equally delicious for your supper tonight.

1 To make the parcels, fry the shallots and garlic in a little oil until soft, then add the cremini mushrooms and cook until soft. Add the assorted mushrooms, nuts, and port and reduce a little. Finally, add the butter, cook for 2 minutes, then remove from the heat and drain for at least 1 hour, or as long as possible.

2 Put a piece of vignotte on each piece of pastry, then top with some of the mushroom mixture. Roll up into a parcel and put on a greased baking sheet. Brush with eggwash, top with sesame seeds and chill for at least 20 minutes.

3 Preheat the oven to 400°F. Cook the parcels for 20 minutes until the pastry is golden.

4 Meanwhile, make the sauce. Heat some oil in a large pan and fry the shallots and garlic for 5 minutes until softened. Add the wine and reduce by half.

5 Chuck in the red peppers and cook for 5 minutes, then add the stock and tarragon and bring to a boil. Cook for 5 minutes, then pour into a food processor and whiz until smooth. Turn out into a dish, season and add a splash of vinegar to cut the sweet sauce.

6 Spoon a little sauce onto each plate, and top with a parcel. Garnish with watercress or other greenery.

2 shallots

1 garlic clove, crushed

7oz cremini mushrooms, cut into bite-sized chunks

29oz assorted mushrooms, cut into bite-sized chunks

1 cup shelled, roasted hazelnuts

splash of port

small piece of cold butter, plus extra for greasing

7oz vignotte cheese

4 x 6inch square pieces puff pastry rolled out to ½inch thick

1 egg, beaten, for eggwash

handful of sesame seeds

olive oil for frying

a little watercress, to garnish (optional)

For the sauce

2 shallots

1 garlic clove

splash of white wine

6 red bell peppers, roasted, skinned, seeded, and chopped

¾ cup stock

sprig of fresh tarragon

splash of white wine vinegar

Sweet potato and pineapple sandwich

Feeds 4

I love sweet potato, it has such a silky smooth texture when it's mashed and a delicious caramel flavor when it's roasted. This dish gets its inspiration from the Caribbean, where there are so many delicious sweet yet savory recipes that it's impossible to be anything other than a complete pig when you visit. You can give this an even bigger Caribbean flavor by adding a slug of rum to the pan when stir-frying the veggies.

1 Preheat the oven to 425°F. Heat the oil in a roasting pan, then add the sweet potato chunks. Season well, give them a good shake and add the chiles, thyme, and garlic. Roast for about 30 minutes until the sweet potato is soft (it's probably worth giving them the odd stir while they're roasting).

2 Brush each of the pineapple slices with oil and cook on a hot griddle pan for a couple of minutes each side until well striped. When they've all been charred, put them in an ovenproof dish with their juice and put to one side.

3 To make the sauce, cook the curry paste in a pan for a few minutes to release the flavor, then add the coconut milk and bring to the boil. Add the stock and cook for 5 minutes.

4 Heat some more oil in a skillet, add the onion and cook until it starts to brown. Add the red pepper and then the sweet potatoes. Cook for 3–4 minutes until the potato starts to break down.

5 Spoon in a little of the curry sauce to bind the mixture, then add the okra and cilantro. Stir it around for another couple of minutes.

6 Pop the pineapple slices in the oven for a few minutes to warm through. Put a slice of pineapple on each plate, then spoon a quarter of the sweet potato mixture on top (if you've got them, use small rings to make it neater). Sit another slice of pineapple on top and drizzle some of the curry sauce around the edge.

½ cup vegetable oil

1½lb golden sweet potatoes, peeled and cut into largish bite-sized chunks

2 small red chiles, chopped

handful of fresh thyme

4 garlic cloves, crushed

1 pineapple, peeled and cut into 8 slices (keep the juice)

1 red onion, sliced

1 red bell pepper, seeded and sliced

3oz blanched okra

freshly chopped cilantro leaves

salt and freshly ground black pepper

For the curry sauce

3 tbsp curry paste (mild or hot, whatever's in the cupboard)

1¾ cups coconut milk

½ cup stock

Cheese sausages
with onion gravy

Makes about 12 sausages

The joy of a good sausage is that fried, fatty quality and a strong mystery seasoning. Veggie sausages are tricky, but after years of trying I think this is a pretty good version—when you break them open they look "fatty" and they taste like a dream.

1 The sausage mix couldn't be easier—just chuck all the ingredients except the oil into a large bowl, season well, get your hands in and mix it all up. When you taste it, I reckon you need to over-season it by about 15 percent, so it's a bit more salty and peppery than you'd normally have—the mixture seems to lose some of its power as it chills and cooks. Chill the mixture for 2 hours.

2 Meanwhile, make the gravy. Heat a little oil in a pan and fry the onions, garlic, and sugar over low heat until golden. Sprinkle on the flour and cook for 3–4 minutes. Add the gravy browning and stock and bring to a boil. Season, then simmer for at least 20 minutes.

3 Mold the chilled sausage mix into sausage shapes—you should get about twelve out of it, depending how big you like your sausage... You can either shallow-fry the sausages in a little oil or deep-fry them in a lot of oil; I think the deep-fry method brings the best out of the flavor and texture. Fry them for about 5 minutes until golden, then drain well on some paper towels and serve with the gravy.

4 This fabulous grub is great with mashed potato (try it with the addition of wholegrain mustard), with a salad, or in a bun smothered in ketchup, onions, and mustard and served with fries.

*If you can find British Lancashire cheese, use instead of the Cheddar.

For the sausages

1lb 5oz Cheddar* cheese, grated
or crumbled

3½ cups fresh breadcrumbs

6 scallions, chopped

2 tbsp fresh thyme, chopped

2 tbsp freshly chopped parsley

3 whole eggs, plus 3 egg yolks

2 garlic cloves, crushed

about 3 tbsp milk, to bind

salt and freshly ground black pepper

vegetable oil for frying

For the onion gravy

3 large onions, sliced

2 garlic cloves, crushed

1 tbsp brown sugar

⅔ cup all-purpose flour

⅓ cup gravy browning

3 cups stock

Penne all'arabiata

Feeds 4

This is one of the simplest pasta dishes in the world and definitely one of the most delicious. It's particularly good if you grow your own tomatoes as their sweet earthiness makes it even better.

1 Cook the pasta in boiling salted water until al dente. Meanwhile, heat the oil in a pan and gently fry the shallots, chiles and garlic until soft, then add the tomatoes and turn up the heat. Once the tomatoes begin to break up, turn down the heat and simmer for about 5 minutes to form a sauce.

2 Drain the pasta over a pan and add to the sauce with a little of the water the pasta was cooked in. Season well and stir in the parsley. Serve with big shavings of Parmesan, crusty bread, and a fruity Valpolicella red wine.

10oz dried penne

½ cup olive oil

2 shallots, finely chopped

2 small red hot chiles, seeded and chopped

1 garlic clove, crushed

8 tomatoes, finely chopped

a good handful of freshly chopped parsley

salt and freshly ground black pepper

Parmesan shavings, to serve

Macaroni cheese

Real comfort food—a bowl of creamy macaroni cheese never fails to hit the spot. In this recipe I've added both cherry and sun-blushed tomatoes to make it more of a sunshine dish. If you pack the mac-cheese into a presentation ring before it goes into the oven you can make it posh enough for an informal lunch/dinner for friends. But if you're doing it for yourself, slap it into a big bowl and wade in.

1 Preheat the oven to 400°F. To make the sauce, pour the milk into a pan, add the bay leaves and heat to scalding point. Remove from the heat and, when cooled a little, discard the bay leaves.

2 Melt the butter in a pan, stir in the flour and cook, stirring, for 3 minutes (don't let it brown). Add a little of the milk to the flour and stir to combine. Cook briefly, then gradually add the rest of the milk and stir until you have a smooth sauce. Bring to the boil, stirring all the time, reduce the heat and simmer for 3 minutes. Take off the heat and stir in the cheese, mustard, and seasoning.

3 Heat the oil in a large pan and fry the shallots until translucent, then add the pasta, all the tomatoes, and the cheese sauce. The sauce should coat, not swamp, the macaroni (you may need to add a little milk to loosen the sauce).

4 Heat through, then pour into an ovenproof dish and sprinkle with Parmesan. Bake in the oven for 6–8 minutes until the sauce begins to thicken.

5 Finish off under a hot broiler, and top with chopped parsley.

2 tbsp olive oil

4 shallots, sliced

14oz cooked macaroni

20 cherry tomatoes, halved

12 sun-blushed tomatoes

freshly grated Parmesan cheese

freshly chopped parsley

For the cheese sauce

2 cups milk

2 bay leaves

¼ stick (2 tbsp) butter

3½ tbsp all-purpose flour

1¼ cups grated mature Cheddar or Gruyère cheese

1 tsp English mustard

salt and freshly ground black pepper

Linguine with potato and pesto

Feeds 4

More comfort food—potato and pasta is a great combination, if you don't feel like it's a carb overload. Add strong pesto and creamy mascarpone and you may never leave the house again.

1 To make the pesto, put all the ingredients except the oil into a blender and blend until smooth. Then, with the motor running, slowly add enough oil to make a thick sauce.

2 Cook the pasta in loads of boiling salted water for about 8 minutes.

3 Very finely dice the potatoes and put in water. Heat the oil in a skillet. Drain and dry the potatoes and fry, stirring continuously, until crisp and golden. Don't allow them to burn. Take them off the heat and drain on paper towels.

4 Drain the cooked pasta, then put it back in the pan. Add all the remaining ingredients and the pesto to the pasta and warm through. Check the seasoning.

5 Serve with black pepper and Parmesan shavings—this is delicious.

14oz dried linguine

2 potatoes, e.g. russet, peeled

3½ tbsp olive oil

2 garlic cloves, crushed

1 x 8oz tub mascarpone cheese

½ cup stock

salt and freshly ground black pepper

Parmesan shavings, to serve

For the pesto

1¾ cups pine nuts

large bunch of fresh basil leaves

1¼ cups freshly grated Parmesan cheese

2 garlic cloves

extra-virgin olive oil

Gnocchi with wild mushroom and rosemary ragu

Feeds 12

Once you've made this dish it will become a firm favorite in your repertoire. It's packed full of flavor, taste, and texture and the smell when you're cooking it is heaven. I reckon this'll feed about 12 of you, but I find if you reduce the quantities it doesn't work as well, so invite all those people round you haven't seen for absolutely ages.

1 To make the gnocchi, boil the potatoes for about 40 minutes until soft. Drain, and when cool enough to handle peel and mash or pass through a ricer into a bowl.

2 Make a well in the center of the mash, add the egg and mix in, then add the flour and seasoning. Mix to form a dough, then knead for a few minutes until dry to the touch.

3 Divide the potato dough into three and roll each out into ¾inch diameter ropes, then cut off at ¾inch intervals. Press one side of each gnocchi with the back of a fork to form "grooves"—this will give the sauce something to stick to.

4 Bring a large pan of water to a boil and drop the gnocchi into the water. When they rise to the top, scoop out and refresh in ice-cold water. Drain well, then pat dry, toss in oil and chill until needed. You can also freeze them at this stage.

5 To make the ragu, heat some oil in a pan and gently fry the vegetables for 5 minutes until soft. Add the tomato paste and cook for 7–8 minutes until a rich red.

6 Add the wine, stock, and rosemary, bring to a boil, then simmer for at least 40 minutes, but preferably 1 hour.

7 When ready to serve, cut the mushrooms into chunks and fry with the garlic in oil until soft, season well.

8 Warm the gnocchi in the ragu, spoon onto a plate and top with the mushrooms and Parmesan.

1½lb floury potatoes, e.g. russet, unpeeled

1 large egg

3½ cups all-purpose flour

salt and freshly ground black pepper

For the ragu

olive oil for frying and tossing

2 onions, finely chopped

2 carrots, finely chopped

2 celery stalks, finely chopped

2 garlic cloves, crushed

10oz tomato paste

3½ cups red wine

3½ cups stock

fresh rosemary to taste

For the topping

1lb Portobello mushrooms

1 garlic clove

freshly grated Parmesan cheese, to serve

Goat's cheese cannelloni with cherry tomatoes

I got a bit fed up with cannelloni baked in either tomato or béchamel sauce, so I started roasting little cherry tomatoes in lots of oil, to make a semi-sauce. This is packed full of flavor and looks divine.

1 Preheat the oven to 425ºF. Pour some oil into a roasting tin and put in the oven to heat up. Chuck the tomatoes into the hot pan and roast for about 10 minutes.

2 Add the thyme, balsamic vinegar, garlic, and seasoning and roast for a further 15 minutes, then remove the pan from the oven and keep warm. Reduce the oven temperature to 350ºF.

3 Make the filling by combining the cheeses and spinach with lots of seasoning in a bowl.

4 Lay the pasta out and put a line of filling along the long edge of each piece, then roll up into a cannelloni shape.

5 Drizzle a little of the oil from the tomatoes on the bottom of an ovenproof dish large enough to hold all 12 cannelloni. Then pack the tubes in and pour the tomatoes over. Bake in the oven for 15 minutes until heated through.

6 Serve topped with shaved Parmesan and a crisp green salad dressed with oil and balsamic vinegar.

14oz cherry tomatoes, halved

fresh thyme

dash of balsamic vinegar

2 garlic cloves, crushed

12 sheets of fresh pasta, 4½ x 4inches square

olive oil for roasting

salt and freshly ground black pepper

Parmesan shavings, to serve

For the filling

1 x 8oz tub ricotta cheese

6oz goat's cheese

1¼ cups freshly grated Parmesan cheese

5–6 cups baby spinach leaves, well washed and drained

Lemon grass risotto
with lime leaf tapenade

Feeds 4 for lunch

As long as you add warm stock to the rice, don't stir it too much and let it know you love it, making risotto is very straightforward. This fragrant variation is delicious—the lemon grass is so uplifting.

1 Fry the shallots and garlic in a little oil until soft. Bruise the lemon grass with the back of a knife and add to the pan. Add the rice and stir gently for a couple of minutes until the edge of the rice becomes translucent. Then add the wine and cook for a minute or two.

2 Add a good ladleful of stock to the rice and cook, stirring, until it has been absorbed. Repeat with more stock until it has all been used and/or the rice is soft. Season well.

3 To make the tapenade, simply put all the ingredients except the oil in a food processor, add seasoning and blend. When it's pretty broken down, leave the motor running and slowly add the oil. Spoon out into a bowl.

4 Add a swirl of cream to the rice just before serving, then divide between four bowls and top each serving with some tapenade.

4 shallots, sliced

1 garlic clove, crushed

3 stalks of lemon grass

2½ cups arborio rice

splash of white wine

2¾ cups stock

splash of cream

vegetable oil for frying

salt and freshly ground black pepper

For the tapenade

8 fresh kaffir lime leaves, torn

⅔ cup green olives, pitted

1 tbsp capers

handful of cilantro stalks

1 garlic clove

juice and zest of 1 lime

⅓ cup olive oil

Moroccan spaghetti

Feeds 4

One of the best places I've been to is Marrakesh—the sights, sounds, smells, and people are so stimulating. The food market at Djemma el-Fna square has some of the best street food anywhere, with its wonderful aromas of cinnamon, almonds, and cumin. So this is inspired by that trip; it's simple pasta with a sauce a-la-Marrakesh.

1 Cook the spaghetti in boiling salted water until al dente.

2 Meanwhile, heat the oil in a pan and gently fry the onion and garlic until soft.

3 Add the tomatoes, cinnamon, cumin, and turmeric and cook over a medium heat for about 20 minutes until the tomatoes break down.

4 Season the sauce and then add the almonds and chickpeas.

5 Drain the pasta and divide between four plates. Fold the herbs into the sauce and mix it with the pasta.

10oz dried spaghetti

½ cup olive oil

1 onion, finely chopped

2 garlic cloves, crushed

8 tomatoes, finely chopped

1 tsp ground cinnamon

1 tsp ground cumin

pinch of turmeric

1 cup toasted, slivered almonds

½ cup cooked chickpeas (garbanzo beans), drained and rinsed if canned

bunch each of fresh parsley and cilantro leaves, finely chopped

handful of freshly chopped mint leaves

salt and freshly ground black pepper

Four-cheese and zucchini penne

Feeds 4

An easy pasta dish that shows how essential it is to use good ingredients in simple dishes. I like to cook the zucchini slowly so they almost begin to "melt." Watch out for the salt—you don't need much at all as the cheeses will provide it.

1 Cook the penne in lots of boiling salted water until al dente.

2 While it is cooking, fry the zucchini and garlic slowly in some oil until very soft. Season to taste.

3 Put all the cheeses in a separate pan with a little splash of oil and slowly warm through until they begin to melt. Add a splash of wine and the zucchini and cook very gently for 4–5 minutes.

4 Drain the pasta over a saucepan, then add the pasta to the zucchini mixture, together with a little of its cooking water.

5 Stir to mix, check the seasoning and turn out into a serving dish. Top with some Parmesan shavings and serve at once.

14oz dried penne

1lb zucchini, washed and cut into rounds

1 garlic clove, chopped

$\frac{1}{2}$ cup mascarpone cheese

$\frac{1}{2}$ cup freshly grated Parmesan cheese

1 cup crumbled Gorgonzola cheese

$\frac{1}{2}$ cup crumbled Dolcelatte cheese

splash of white wine

olive oil for frying

salt and freshly ground black pepper

Parmesan shavings, to serve

Eggplant tikka masala

Feeds 6

Apparently, chicken tikka masala is now the UK's favorite dish, more than roast dinner and more than fish and chips. If that's the case, then I feel it's only right and proper for there to be a vegetarian version.

1 Toss the eggplants in vegetable oil and salt. Cook on a hot griddle pan until striped on each side.

2 Combine all the marinade ingredients in a bowl, season with salt and coat the eggplant pieces well. Thread onto wooden skewers, put in a sheet, cover and chill for at least 2 hours.

3 Meanwhile, make the sauce. Put the onion, garlic, and chiles in a food processor and blend until smooth. Heat the peanut oil in a pan and fry the onion paste over a low heat for about 7 minutes until golden brown.

4 Roughly chop the cilantro leaves and put with the ginger and tomatoes in the processor (don't bother washing it out) and blend until smooth.

5 Once the onions are golden, spoon the tomato mixture into the pan and cook for a good 15 minutes, until most of the liquid has evaporated.

6 Stir in the ground coriander, cumin, paprika, fenugreek, and garam masala and add salt to taste. Cook briefly, then gently stir in the yogurt, a little at a time, to avoid curdling.

7 Add the milk, crank the heat right up and bring to a boil. Simmer for 5 minutes.

8 Cook the eggplant skewers under a hot broiler, basting with the butter and lemon juice and turning when golden. (They are delicious eaten just like this with a naan bread wrapped around them.)

9 Lay 2 skewers of eggplant tikka on a plate, spoon over some sauce and garnish with cilantro leaves. Serve with rice, naan bread, and icy cold beer.

4–6 eggplants (about 2lb total weight), cut into chunks or wedges
vegetable oil
$3\frac{1}{2}$ tbsp melted butter
juice of 1 lemon
salt
fresh cilantro leaves, to garnish

For the marinade

$\frac{1}{2}$ cup plain yoghurt
juice of 1 lime
2 garlic cloves, crushed
1inch piece of fresh ginger, finely chopped
1 tbsp ground coriander
1 tsp each of ground cumin, garam masala, paprika

For the sauce

1 onion, roughly chopped
5 garlic cloves
3–5 red chiles (seeded if you like)
3 tbsp peanut oil
1 bunch of fresh cilantro leaves
$1\frac{1}{2}$inch piece of fresh ginger
5 plum tomatoes
1 tbsp ground coriander, 2 tsp ground cumin, 1 tsp paprika, 2 tsp ground fenugreek, 1 tsp garam masala
$\frac{1}{3}$ cup plain yoghurt
$\frac{2}{3}$ cup milk

Rendang shallot and asparagus curry

Feeds 6

I first ate rendang in Holland—Amsterdam, where there's a large Malaysian community—it was a knockout: sweet, but not too sweet, spicy, but not too spicy. It's traditionally served with buffalo, slow-cooked to tenderize the meat, and quite dry. Well, I've teamed it with shallots and asparagus and left it a bit wetter, but to be more authentic you can reduce the sauce down.

1 Melt the butter in a pan, add the sugar and when it begins to dissolve chuck in the whole shallots. Season, turn down the heat and cook for at least 45 minutes, turning every 10 minutes or so until the shallots are golden and soft.

2 Blanch the asparagus in boiling salted water, then refresh in ice-cold water.

3 To make the paste, put all the ingredients except the oil in a food processor and blend until smooth.

4 Heat the oil in a wok and fry the paste until fragrant—be careful not to burn it.

5 Add the shredded coconut and the coconut milk, and stir well. Bring to a boil and boil to reduce the sauce by half.

6 Add the shallots, asparagus, and toasted coconut and warm through.

7 Garnish with the cilantro and serve with jasmine rice.

½ stick (4 tbsp) butter
½ cup brown sugar
20 shallots
1lb bundle asparagus, trimmed
2 cups shredded unsweetened coconut
1¾ cups canned coconut milk
⅔ cup desiccated coconut, toasted
vegetable oil for frying
salt and freshly ground black pepper
freshly chopped cilantro leaves and jasmine rice, to serve

For the paste

1 onion, roughly chopped
2 garlic cloves
1inch piece of fresh ginger
3 red chiles (seeded if you like)
1 tsp ground coriander
1 tbsp tamarind paste
1 tsp turmeric
1½ tsp curry powder
1 stalk of lemon grass
pinch of salt
2 tbsp vegetable oil for frying

Italian bean casserole

Feeds 6–8

I think there's something very sexy about this dish; we always imagine casseroles to be heavy and robust, but this one has a lightness with a simple tomato base, lots of beans and lemon. Topped with arancini it's hardcore.

1 Heat some oil in a large casserole, add the carrots, celery and leeks and fry for 3–4 minutes. Season and add the garlic and wine. Let the wine cook out and reduce by two-thirds.

2 Tip in the tomatoes and lemon zest and bring to a boil.

3 Add the stock, bring back to a boil and simmer for 20 minutes.

4 Chuck in the beans and cook for 5 minutes, then add the fresh herbs and the lemon juice. It's worth having a quick recheck of the seasoning now.

5 To make the arancini, roll the risotto into 1½inch balls, press a little cheese into the center and fold to enclose. Deep-fry in hot oil until golden. Drain on paper towels.

6 Serve a good bowlful of casserole with arancini and a little shaved Parmesan on top.

4 carrots, chopped

4 celery stalks, chopped

3 leeks, trimmed, well washed and chopped

2 garlic cloves, crushed

good glug of white wine

15oz can chopped tomatoes

juice and zest of 1 lemon

¾ cup fresh stock

½ cup each of cooked borlotti and cannellini beans, drained and rinsed if canned

fresh oregano

fresh marjoram

olive oil for frying

salt and freshly ground black pepper

Parmesan shavings, to serve

For the arancini

1 quantity cooked tomato risotto (see tomato and mozzarella cakes, page 16)

4oz mozzarella cheese

vegetable oil for deep-frying

Red Thai bean curry

Once you've mastered the art of making your own Thai curry paste you'll never buy it again. It takes a bit of marketing to get all the gear at first, but most of the big supermarkets sell Thai ingredients now, even fresh lime leaves. You won't need all the curry paste, so keep it in an airtight jar in the fridge. Incidentally, try adding a dollop of the paste to creamy mashed potato—divine.

1 To make the curry paste, dry-fry the peppercorns, cumin, and coriander seeds until fragrant, then grind them in a mortar and pestle. Put them with all the other paste ingredients except the oil into a blender and blitz until smooth—it takes a good 5–10 minutes.

2 Warm the oil in a pan and add four good spoonfuls of paste (one per person). Cook on a low heat until it becomes fragrant.

3 Crank up the heat and add the coconut milk and stock and bring to the boil. Boil for 3 minutes.

4 Add the fine green and fava beans, onions, and tomatoes and simmer for about 4 minutes.

5 Divide the luscious curry between four bowls and garnish with lime wedges and cilantro and serve with rice.

1¾ cups canned coconut milk
½ cup stock
8oz cooked fine green beans
8oz cooked fava beans
1 bunch of scallions, finely chopped
2 tomatoes, chopped
lime wedges and fresh cilantro leaves, to serve

For the curry paste

10 black peppercorns
2 tsp cumin seeds
2 tsp coriander seeds
10 red chiles (seeded if you like)
5 shallots
2 garlic cloves, crushed
piece of fresh ginger
6 stalks of lemon grass
12 kaffir lime leaves
pinch of ground cinnamon
½ tsp turmeric
splash of vegetable oil
splash of chili oil
1 tbsp palm sugar
salt
2 tbsp vegetable oil for frying

Black bean and eggplant chili

Feeds 6

You don't expect to see eggplants in a chili, but their meaty texture together with the strong taste of the black beans and the sneaky addition of chocolate make it a delicious combo.

1 Heat the oil in a pan and fry the eggplants for about 4 minutes, to color and soften. Remove and drain on paper towels.

2 Fry the onions and garlic in the same pan until soft, then add the chiles and cook for 5 minutes.

3 Add the tomatoes, coriander, cumin, cinnamon, bay leaf, and eggplants and simmer for 5 minutes.

4 Add the beans, season well and cook for 15 minutes. Stir in the chocolate and serve with grated cheese and/or sour cream.

½ cup vegetable oil

1lb eggplants, cut into 1inch cubes

2 red onions, finely chopped

4 garlic cloves, crushed

10 small red chiles, chopped (seeded if you like)

4 cups canned chopped tomatoes

1 tsp ground coriander

pinch of ground cumin

pinch of ground cinnamon

1 bay leaf

9oz cooked black beans, drained and rinsed if canned

2 tbsp grated best-quality dark chocolate (not unsweetened)

vegetable oil for frying

salt and freshly ground black pepper

grated cheese and/or sour cream, to serve

Ojja with sweet potato and okra

Feeds 6

This is one of the most bizarre success stories on recent menus. This weird little African dish managed to get voted onto the menu in the absence of anything else we could agree on, and it has been really popular. It's got a heady aroma from the smoked paprika and it gets finished with beaten egg, which makes it really creamy.

1 Preheat the oven to 400°F. Pour some oil in a baking tin and put in the oven to heat up. Put the sweet potato with lots of salt and pepper into the hot oil and roast for about 25 minutes until soft and slightly crisp.

2 Meanwhile, make the ojja. Fry the onions and garlic in oil with some seasoning. When they're soft add a splosh of wine and reduce by two-thirds, then add the paprika and cook for about 3 minutes, stirring all the time.

3 Add the tomato paste and stir for a few minutes, then chuck in the tomatoes and bring to a boil. Pour in the stock and cook for about 25 minutes over a low heat until thickened and reduced. Check the seasoning.

4 Blanch the okra and the beans in boiling water, then refresh in ice-cold water.

5 Cook the rice with the turmeric and some salt according to the packet instructions.

6 Heat some oil in a large skillet, add the potatoes and cook until they start to color up, then add the beans, okra, and ojja and bring to the boil. Beat the eggs, add to the pan and let it begin to cook, then fold it through the mixture and keep folding until it creates a lovely marbled effect through the dish.

7 Just before serving, throw in a load of chopped parsley. The texture should be thick enough so you can spoon this up high, it shouldn't be a sloppy casserole. Serve with rice.

2 golden sweet potatoes, peeled and cut into largish bite-sized pieces

3oz fresh okra

4oz fresh fava beans

2¾ cups long-grain rice, rinsed and drained

1 tsp turmeric

2 eggs

lots of freshly chopped parsley

olive oil for frying

salt and freshly ground black pepper

For the ojja

2 onions, sliced

3 garlic cloves, crushed

splash of red wine

1 heaped tbsp smoked paprika—it really needs the smoked stuff, unsmoked doesn't do it

1 tbsp tomato paste

2 cups canned chopped tomatoes

⅔ cup stock

Plantain and mango curry

I can't decide when the best time to eat this dish is—it's a neat little lunchy treat, but also great for party food, and really different because it's bright yellow, and nearly sweet enough for a dessert. Anyway try it with fresh warm naan bread—and friends.

1 Slice the plantain into pieces about ⅛inch thick. Place in a pan of boiling salted water with half the turmeric and cook for 10 minutes, then drain.

2 Fry the nigella or mustard seeds in a little oil until they pop, then add the onion, red chile, curry leaves, and some salt. Cook for 5 minutes over medium heat, stirring pretty much all the time until the onion is golden.

3 Add the ginger and green chile and cook for 1 minute.

4 Add the rest of the turmeric and mix well, then take off the heat and slowly fold in the yogurt, plantain, and mango.

5 Put back on the heat for 1 minute. Serve with rice or naan bread.

1 plantain, not too ripe, peeled

2 tsp turmeric

1 tsp nigella seeds (or black mustard seeds)

1 onion, finely sliced

1 dried red chile

about 25 curry leaves

1inch piece of fresh ginger, finely chopped

1 fresh green chile, seeded and sliced

1¾ cups plain yoghurt

1 firm mango, peeled and sliced

vegetable oil for frying

salt

Oriental pie

Feeds 6

Sounds strange, cooks up a storm. This is really a shepherd's pie-style dish. Big strong mushroom flavors, enhanced by oriental spices and topped with a very Western, creamy mash topping. You can substitute pretty much any favorite earthy veg for the mushrooms.

1 Fry the scallions in a little oil until they wilt. Add all the mushrooms to the pan and cook for 5 minutes, then add the garlic, ginger, cinnamon, and star anise and cook for 5 minutes more.

2 Add the soy sauce and stock and bring to a boil, then simmer for about 10 minutes to reduce by half.

3 Preheat the oven to 400°F. Pour the mushroom mixture into a baking dish and add the chickpeas.

4 To make the topping, put both mashed potatoes into a pan and stir to combine. Beat in the butter and cream and season well, then warm through over low heat.

5 Spoon the mash on top of the mushroom and chickpea mixture and cook in the oven for 15 minutes. Finish off under the broiler to brown the top.

8 scallions, left whole

9oz Portobello mushrooms, halved

7oz shiitake mushrooms

1 garlic clove, crushed

1inch piece of fresh ginger, sliced into matchsticks

1 cinnamon stick

2 star anise

½ cup light soy sauce

½ cup stock

¾ cup cooked chickpeas (garbanzo beans), rinsed and drained if canned

vegetable oil for frying

For the topping

1 cup mashed potato

1 cup mashed sweet potato

1¼ sticks (10 tbsp) butter

3½ tbsp heavy cream

salt and freshly ground black pepper

Caramelized onion and mustard tart

Feeds 6

A big "meaty" dish that's great for lunch, with sweet, strong onions, the sharpness of the mustard and crisp shortcrust pastry. I serve this with a tomato salad or chutney.

1 Roll out the pastry on a lightly floured surface to fit a 8–10inch tart pan, press into the pan and chill for 20 minutes.

2 Preheat the oven to 400°F. Bake the pastry case for 25–30 minutes until crisp and dry.

3 Meanwhile, melt the butter and oil together over a low heat, then add the onions, garlic, and seasoning. Cook the onions very slowly for 30–40 minutes until golden—don't let them burn.

4 Whisk together the whole eggs, egg yolks, mustard, and cream and stir in the cooked onions. Remove the tart case from the oven and reduce the heat to 350°F. Spoon the filling into the tart case and bake for 20 minutes until set firm and golden.

1 quantity shortcrust pastry (see below)

flour for dusting

½ stick (4 tbsp) butter

1 tbsp vegetable oil

4 large Spanish onions, sliced

1 garlic clove, crushed

2 whole eggs, plus 2 egg yolks

2 tbsp wholegrain mustard

⅔ cup heavy cream

salt and freshly ground black pepper

Shortcrust pastry

Makes enough for 1 x 10inch pie dish

1 Put the flour, butter and salt in a food processor and pulse until "crumby". Add the milk and egg yolk and pulse until a dough forms.

2 Turn the dough out onto a lightly floured surface and knead for a few minutes, then cover and chill for at least 1 hour.

3 When you're ready to use it, roll the dough out on a floured surface and use as directed.

1¾ cups all-purpose flour, plus extra for dusting

¾ stick (6 tbsp) chilled butter, cubed

pinch of salt

3½ tbsp milk

1 egg yolk

Jerk-spiced
pumpkin pie

Feeds 6

Remember eating loads of vol-au-vents filled with mushrooms at parties? You know they're corny, and that mushroom filling is vile, but you can't help yourself. Well, this is Mr vol-au-vent's cooler elder brother, he's bigger, tastier and a whole lot more handsome.

1 Preheat the oven to 375ºF. Cut a 3inch circle out of the middle of six of the pastry circles. Put the whole pastry circles on a floured baking sheet and sit a cut one on top of each. Brush with eggwash and bake for about 20 minutes until golden brown and dry. Remove the pie cases from the oven.

2 For the filling, pour some oil in a roasting pan and heat to smoking, either in the oven or on the hob. Throw in the squash (not literally!) and shake around for a couple of minutes, then sprinkle on the jerk seasoning and mix well. Roast in the oven for about 25 minutes until soft with a little crispness on the outside. Remove from the pan and put to one side. Pour the oil into a skillet and fry the spinach and almonds, then season and add to the squash. Divide the fillling between the pie cases and warm through in the oven for 5 minutes.

3 For the curry sauce, heat the oil in a pan and fry the paste until fragrant, then add the coconut milk and stock, bring to a boil and simmer for 5 minutes.

4 Fry the plantain slices gently in oil until golden on each side, then put aside and keep them warm.

5 Sit a pie on each plate, spoon over just enough sauce to cover the ingredients, not to swamp them, top with a few slices of the plantain and garnish with cilantro.

12 x 6inch circles of ready-rolled puff pastry
flour for dusting
2 eggs, beaten, for eggwash
2 plantain, peeled and sliced
vegetable oil for roasting and frying
fresh cilantro leaves, to garnish

For the filling

1½lb butternut squash, peeled and cubed
3 heaped tbsp jerk seasoning
a handful of spinach leaves, well washed and drained
1 cup toasted slivered almonds
salt and freshly ground black pepper

For the curry sauce

1 tbsp vegetable oil
3 heaped tbsp mild curry paste
1¾ cups canned coconut milk
½ cup stock

Stilton, asparagus and caramelized shallot roulade with spicy chutney

Feeds 4

This roulade couldn't be more different in flavors than the following one. I've served it with a pear chutney, but I think it's a good dish for Christmas, so try adding a few fresh cranberries to the chutney.

1 First make the roulade. Melt the butter in a pan and stir in the flour to make a roux. Cook for 3 minutes, then add the milk, a little at a time, and stir until thickened. Season well, then stir in the egg yolks. Take off the heat and leave to cool. When cooled, stir in the spinach. Beat the egg whites until stiff then gently fold into the mixture.

2 Preheat the oven to 400°F. Grease and line a 15 x 10inch baking sheet and sprinkle with flour. Spoon the mixture onto the sheet and cook for about 15 minutes until firm and springy. Turn out onto a piece of waxed paper, carefully remove the lining paper and leave to cool.

3 For the filling, heat the butter in a pan and when bubbling add the shallots, season well and simmer on a very low heat for 30–40 minutes until rich and golden. Stir frequently to stop them burning. Spread the cream cheese evenly over each cooled roulade, then sprinkle on the Stilton, shallots, nuts, and asparagus.

4 Using the waxed paper to help you, roll the roulade up from one long side, then wrap in waxed paper and foil and chill overnight.

5 To make the chutney, heat a little oil in a pan and fry the shallots and garlic until soft. Add the pears and ginger and cook for 5 minutes, then add the vinegar, sugar, and chile and cook over a low heat for about 20 minutes. Season to taste, then set aside to cool.

6 When ready to serve, preheat the oven to 400°F. Cut the roulade into 8 slices and put on a baking sheet. Cook for about 10 minutes until they begin to crisp and brown. Serve the roulade with the chutney and some wilted spinach.

½ stick + 1 tbsp (5 tbsp) butter, plus extra for greasing

⅞ cup all-purpose flour, plus extra for dusting

1¾ cups warmed milk

7 eggs, separated

handful of freshly chopped spinach leaves

salt and freshly ground black pepper

For the filling

½ stick (4 tbsp) butter

15 shallots, sliced

1 cup soft cream cheese

6oz Stilton cheese, crumbled

½ cup walnut halves

about 10 asparagus spears, halved lengthways

For the chutney

olive oil for frying

2 shallots, chopped

1 garlic clove, crushed

6 unpeeled pears, cored and chopped

¼ cup chopped preserved ginger

½ cup white wine vinegar

6 tbsp superfine sugar

1 chile, finely chopped

Basil roulade with goat's cheese and sun-blushed tomatoes

Feeds 4

A particularly popular dish whenever it's on the menu at Greens. The combination of goat's cheese, sun-blushed tomatoes and basil makes everyone think of the Mediterranean. But just so you don't get too carried away, some good old beets will bring you back to earth.

Make these roulades a day in advance, so they get a chance to firm up. This is a lovely dish to serve for a special occasion.

1 First make the roulade. Melt the butter in a pan and stir in the flour to make a roux. Cook for 3 minutes, then add the milk, a little at a time, and stir until thickened. Season well, then stir in the egg yolks. Take off the heat and leave to cool.

2 Beat the egg whites until stiff, then gently and carefully fold into the cooled mixture, keeping in as much air as possible. Then gently fold in the basil.

3 Preheat the oven to 400°F. Grease and line a 15 x 10inch baking sheet. Spread the mixture onto the sheet, top with the Parmesan and cook for 15 minutes until springy and risen. Turn out onto a piece of waxed paper, carefully remove the lining paper and leave to cool.

4 To make the filling, season the ricotta cheese and spread some on the cooled roulade base, leaving a gap at each end, then sprinkle on the goat's cheese, basil, and tomatoes. Roll the roulade up from one long side, then wrap in waxed paper and foil and chill overnight.

5 When ready to serve, preheat the oven to 400°F. Slice the roulade, allowing two wedges per person, and heat in the oven for about 10 minutes, then finish off under a hot broiler to crisp slightly. Transfer to a serving plate with some watercress or other greenery.

6 Meanwhile, make the beet caviar. Heat the oil in a pan and fry the shallots, garlic, and lime leaves until soft, then add the beets and warm through. Put into a food processor and pulse until broken down but still a little chunky. Serve with the roulade.

½ stick + 1 tbsp (5 tbsp) butter, plus extra for greasing

⅞ cup all-purpose flour

1¾ cups milk, warmed

7 eggs, separated

big handful of roughly chopped fresh basil leaves

¾ cup freshly grated Parmesan cheese

salt and freshly ground black pepper

watercress, to serve (optional)

For the filling

1 x 8oz tub ricotta cheese

1 cup crumbled goat's cheese

big handful of fresh basil leaves

sprinkle of sun-blushed tomatoes

For the beet caviar

2 tbsp olive oil

2 shallots, finely chopped

1 garlic clove, crushed

4 lime leaves, shredded

6 cooked beets, peeled and chopped

Side dishes

Bubble and squeak

Feeds 4

I've heard rumors of people using cabbage, rather than sprouts, in their bubble… you, of course, would never dream of such a barbaric act. Long live the sprouts!

1 Fry the onions in half the butter until soft, but not colored. Leave to cool.

2 Combine the onions with the potatoes, sprouts, and garlic and season well (heavy on the pepper).

3 Divide the mix into four and shape into squares or rounds. Dust with a little flour and fry in the remaining butter for about 5 minutes on each side until golden.

2 onions, sliced
½ stick (4 tbsp) butter
1 cup mashed potatoes (no butter or cream)
1–1½ cups cooked sprouts
1 garlic clove, crushed
a little flour for dusting
salt and freshly ground black pepper

Pan haggerty

Feeds 4

I hope this version of the classic north-east England potato dish is accurate, otherwise Scotty and all my Geordie mates will never forgive me. It's a great side dish for a lazy Sunday supper.

1 Preheat the oven to 350ºF. Heat half the butter in an ovenproof pan and fry the onion until soft, then remove from the pan.

2 Put a layer of potato in the same pan and fry for a few minutes until golden.

3 Now layer up onion, potato, onion, seasoning each layer and finishing with potato.

4 Melt the remaining butter and pour over the pan. Cook in the oven for about 40 minutes until soft.

5 Before serving, grate the cheese over the top and put under a hot broiler until the cheese bubbles.

½ stick (4 tbsp) butter
1 onion, finely sliced
7oz (about 1 fist-sized) waxy potato, peeled and finely sliced
3oz mature Cheddar cheese
salt and freshly ground black pepper

Lentils with lemon

So often lentils get overcooked and taste of nothing, but this dish uses Puy lentils, which are a lovely green lentil when cooked, but a bluey/purple when raw. Adding lemon and red bell peppers makes this a yummy dish to serve on the side of just about everything savory.

1 Boil the lentils for 10 minutes in lots of boiling salted water. Drain.

2 Bring the stock to a boil and add the lentils and garlic. When it returns to the boil chuck in the lemon juice, zest, and the peppers. Adjust the seasoning and serve immediately.

1 cup Puy lentils
½ cup stock
1 garlic clove, crushed
juice and zest of 1 lemon
½ red bell pepper, seeded and finely diced
salt and freshly ground black pepper

Smoky roasties

Enough for you—and 3 others

You can't beat a good roastie, crisp on the outside, fluffy on the inside and nice and salty. Well, these chaps are so good you can eat them on their own. I'd keep these a secret from all of your friends, otherwise you'll become a roast potato factory.

1 Preheat the oven to 425°F. Pour the oil into an ovenproof dish and heat to smoking in the oven.

2 Cut the potatoes into big chunks, about 2inch-ish in an abstract way. Boil them for 4 minutes in salted water, then drain and return them to the pan. Pop them back on the heat and give them a good shake (this will break up the edges and give them that crispy/fluffy look) for a minute or so.

3 Remove the hot oil from the oven, lift the potatoes out of the pan, ignoring all the small "crumbs," and pop them into the oil. Put them straight in the oven and cook, turning them every 10–15 minutes, for 30 minutes until crisp and golden.

4 Just before serving, season them with salt, sprinkle on the paprika, give 'em another gentle shake and serve.

⅔ cup olive oil
4–6 large, floury potatoes, peeled
sea salt
good pinch of smoked paprika

Sprouts with beet

Feeds 4

Two of the most maligned and underrated veggies in the world. Sprouts aren't just for Christmas and beets aren't just to be pickled in a jar. The combination of these two is heavenly—sweet, sharp, and with garlic and chili thrown in. Don't be afraid, try them.

1 Preheat the oven to 400°F. Season the beets, wrap them in foil and roast for about 40 minutes until soft. Allow to cool, then peel them and cut into wedges.

2 If the sprouts are big, cut them in half, if not, leave them whole.

3 Heat the oil in a skillet until hot. Simply chuck in the sprouts, let them fry for a minute to begin browning, then give them a shake.

4 Now put the beets, chili flakes, and garlic into the pan. Cook for a couple of minutes, then season really well.

5 Serve as a funky veg.

2 raw beets
1½–2 cups cooked sprouts
a little olive oil for frying
pinch of chili flakes
1 garlic clove, crushed
salt and freshly ground black pepper

Glazed carrots with caraway seeds

Feeds 4

If you're bored with carrots, then tuck into these tasty, sweet little beauties.

1 Pop the carrots in a pan with a good pinch of salt and just cover them with water. Add the sugar, caraway, and butter, bring to a boil and simmer for 8–10 minutes, until just tender, but with a bite.

2 Drain the liquid into another pan and reduce by about two-thirds.

3 Add the carrots and caraway to the pan, season and serve.

1lb peeled carrots, cut into batons
1 tsp sugar
1 tsp caraway seeds
3 tbsp butter
salt and freshly ground black pepper

Stuffed pimentos with thyme and basil

Feeds 4

If you're serving something quite plain, then these sweet, slightly spicy peppers are a great accompaniment. Because they get charred and the thyme and basil are pretty strong they make the most boring dish spring to life.

1 Heat a griddle pan to smoking hot and brush it with a tiny amount of oil. Griddle the peppers on both sides until lightly charred. Meanwhile, mix together the ricotta, thyme, lemon juice, and seasoning.

2 While the peppers are still warm, roughly spread a spoonful of the mix onto each pepper. Sit the peppers side by side on a plate, sprinkle a few basil leaves on top and serve (if you want a bit more spice, drizzle a little chili oil over the peppers before serving).

a little vegetable or olive oil for griddling

6 long thin red pimento peppers, halved lengthwise and seeded

¾ cup ricotta cheese

small bunch of fresh thyme

juice of ½ lemon

a few fresh basil leaves

salt and freshly ground black pepper

Celeriac and potato dauphinoise

Feeds 6

It's a grand tradition Chez Rimmer to have dauphinoise potatoes to excess at Christmas time, so imagine everyone's surprise when that tasty, yet ugly veg the celeriac joined the celebrations. But let me tell you, he was a most welcome guest after the first large mouthful as celeriac is a brilliant addition to your creamy dauphinoise.

1 Heat the butter in a pan and gently fry the onion and garlic until soft, but not brown. Reserve a little of the cheese, then layer up the potatoes, celeriac, remaining cheese, and onion in a buttered baking dish, seasoning each layer as you go. Combine the creams and season well, then pour into the dish and leave to stand for about 20 minutes.

2 Preheat the oven to 325°F. Sprinkle the dish with the reserved cheese, then cook the dauphinoise for about 1½ hours until soft.

¼ stick (2 tbsp) butter, plus extra for greasing

1 onion, finely sliced

1 garlic clove, crushed

1½ cups grated mature Cheddar cheese

1lb floury potatoes, peeled and finely sliced

1lb celeriac (celery root), peeled and finely sliced

1¼ cups heavy cream

1¼ cups light cream

salt and freshly ground black pepper

Parmesan-roasted parsnips

I adore all roasted veg, but parsnips are just about my faves. Adding strong Parmesan and garlic makes them good enough to eat on their own—so if you're serving these as a veg with your roast make twice the amount because you'll eat half of them before they get to the table.

1 Preheat the oven to 425°F. Pour some oil into a roasting pan and put in the oven to heat up. Toss the parsnips in the garlic and seasoning.

2 When the oil is smoking, add the parsnips to the pan and roast for about 25 minutes, shaking occasionally (that's the parsnips, not you).

3 Then add the cheese and roast for another 10 minutes. The cheese will begin to melt and form a yummy, stringy coating.

4 Serve the parsnips topped with a twist of black pepper and a little chopped parsley.

14oz parsnips, peeled and cut into 2inch batons

1 garlic clove, sliced

1½ cups freshly grated Parmesan cheese

olive oil for roasting

salt and freshly ground black pepper

freshly chopped parsley, to serve

Fine green beans with garlic and tomato sauce

Fine green beans are one of the few veg that I like cooked slowly; they become deliciously sweet and scrummy. Add a touch of cinnamon to the tomato sauce for an extra flavor.

1 Preheat the oven to 325°F. Cook the green beans in boiling salted water for about 4 minutes, then refresh in ice-cold water.

2 Heat the oil in an ovenproof dish, add the garlic and as soon as it begins to "fizz" add the beans and tomato sauce. Season well and stir to mix, then cook in the oven for 25 minutes until the beans are soft and sweet.

1lb fine green beans

½ cup olive oil

4 garlic cloves, sliced

1 cup basic tomato sauce (see page 107)

salt and freshly ground black pepper

Coconut rice in banana leaf

Feeds 6

There's a good few curries in the book, so this is a simple, yet effective way to serve rice. Good to put on the barbie as well.

1 Put the rice in a pan with the water and coconut cream. Bring to a boil and cook for about 12 minutes.

2 Take it off the heat and stir in the chiles. Divide between the banana leaves, top with some cilantro and wrap the leaves up. Secure the leaf parcels with a skewer then put in a steamer and steam for another 5 minutes.

* If you can't find block coconut cream, lift the solid cream off the surface of canned cocnut milk.

$1\frac{1}{4}$ cups long-grain rice, rinsed and drained

2 cups water

8oz block coconut cream, chopped*

2 small red chiles, seeded and sliced

6 pieces banana leaf, about 12 x 8inches

fresh cilantro leaves

Basic tomato sauce

Makes enough sauce for 4 large bowls of pasta

I prefer this slightly heavier tomato sauce for my dishes as that little bit of extra depth helps with a lot of veggie food. I recommend making twice this amount if you use it on a regular basis, as you can freeze it and use at a later date.

1 Heat the oil in a large pan and gently fry the onion, celery, and garlic until soft.

2 Add the tomato paste and cook for a few minutes, then add the tomatoes, stock and wine. Season and bring to a boil.

3 Turn the heat right down, half cover the pan and simmer for about 1 hour, stirring every now and again.

4 If you want a nice smooth sauce blend in a processor and pass through a fine sieve before using, otherwise use as is.

$\frac{1}{2}$ cup olive oil

1 onion, chopped

1 celery stalk, finely chopped

2 garlic cloves, chopped

2 tbsp tomato paste

4 cups canned chopped tomatoes

$\frac{1}{2}$ cup stock

$\frac{1}{2}$ cup red wine

salt and freshly ground black pepper

Desserts

Popsicles

Remember when you were a kid and you made simple popsicles from cheap orange drink that was always a bit too strong, so it made you cough? Well, now is the time to rediscover your childhood and make these two yummy popsicles that kids will love, but that are also a great fun thing to have at a summer party. Serve them in a bowl of ice with the sticks pointing up.

Watermelon and lime

Makes 8 popsicles

Put the sugar, water and vanilla seeds into a pan and heat until the sugar dissolves, then cool and chill until really cold. Stir in the watermelon and lime juices, pour into eight lolly moulds and freeze. Don't forget the sticks.

½ cup + 1 tbsp superfine sugar

½ cup water

seeds of 1 vanilla bean

2½ cups watermelon juice (squeeze out some watermelon pulp)

juice of 2 limes

Strawberry and black pepper popsicle

Makes 8 popsicles

Simply blend the yogurt, fruit, and sugar together, then add a good twist of pepper. Pour into molds and freeze. Don't forget the sticks.

1¼ cups plain yogurt

4oz strawberries, hulled

4 tbsp caster sugar

freshly ground black pepper

Honeycomb ice cream

The taste of honeycomb/cinder toffee is divine, a real taste of childhood, and I even like the 3 hours it takes to pick the bits out of my teeth. Well, it's only very recently that I learned how to make it and now I can't stop, much to the delight of my dentist, Roger.

If you've tried making ice cream before and been disappointed by the results because it's too "icy," well this is a creamy winner—the secret ingredient is vodka, which has a lower freezing point and stops those ice-crystals forming. Now, where did I put that toothpick?

1 To make the honeycomb, put the sugar and syrup into a pan and warm until the sugar dissolves, then turn up the heat until it starts to form a caramel. The longer you leave it the more caramelly it becomes, but don't leave it too long as it'll burn. You want it golden.

2 Now, chuck in the bicarbonate of soda and stir well, then pour onto a greased tray and allow to cool (how easy is that?).

3 For the ice cream, whip the cream until it becomes thick, but not fully whipped. Fold in the vodka and condensed milk and whisk until firm, then break in the honeycomb and mix well. Pour into a freezer container and freeze for at least 8 hours—there's no need to churn.

For the honeycomb

6 tbsp superfine sugar

2 tbsp English golden syrup or corn syrup

2 tbsp bicarbonate of soda, sifted

For the ice cream

1 pint heavy cream

3 tbsp vodka

¾ cup sweetened condensed milk

Strawberry soup

Feeds 4–6

This is a really lovely summer dessert, full of flavour and color. The best way to describe the taste is like a good snog!—and your lips tingle afterwards.

1 Put 1¾lb of the strawberries and all the superfine sugar in a food processor and process to a purée. Pass through a strainer into a serving bowl and stir in the wine.

2 Add the nectarines, raspberries, and the pulp from the passion fruit and stir to mix.

3 Cover and chill until lovely and cold.

4 Serve each helping with a quenelle of mascarpone and fresh mint leaves.

2¼lb strawberries, hulled

6 tbsp superfine sugar

½ cup dessert wine

2 nectarines, peeled and diced

9oz raspberries, halved

4 passion fruit, halved

½ an 8oz tub mascarpone cheese

mint leaves, to garnish

Strawberry, vodka and black pepper granita

Feeds 6

This isn't really a dessert but I wanted to include it as it's a great drink to start or end a summer evening with—fruity, boozy, and refreshing, and lethal!

1 Heat the sugar and water in a pan over low heat until the sugar dissolves, then take off the heat and chill.

2 Blend the chilled syrup with the fuit, booze, and pepper.

3 Pour into a freezer container, then put in the freezer.

4 Break up the ice crystals every 40 minutes until the granita is completely frozen and has a grainy consistency.

5 Serve in chilled stem glasses with more fruit and mint.

2⅔ cups superfine sugar

2 cups water

10oz strawberries, plus extra to decorate

½ cup vodka

good twist black pepper

fresh mint leaves, to garnish

Strawberry and coconut trifle

Makes 6 individual or 1 big trifle

I love trifle, it always reminds me of big family parties when I was a kid. You just can't beat sherry-soaked cake, trapped inside jello with a big load of tinned fruit, topped with custard, cream and then decorated with hundreds and thousands and those little silver balls that break your teeth in half. Now this trifle is so gorgeous you'll want to stick pictures of it in a scrapbook and send it fan mail. Making custard with coconut milk really is spectacular, while soaking fat juicy strawberries in Cointreau is making me salivate as I write. Anyway, to the recipe.

This does take a bit of time as you've got to make the custard and then let it cool, so if you're thinking of making it for supper tonight, better eat late.

1 First make the custard. Whisk the egg yolks and sugar until they're pale and creamy, then sift in the flour and mix well. Put the coconut milk and vanilla seeds into another pan and very slowly bring it to a boil (if you want a really thick custard use just the top solid part of the coconut milk, you'll need 2 cans). When it's come to a boil, take it off the heat, pour over the egg mixture and whisk well. Pour it all back into the pan and bring back up to a boil, then simmer for 5 minutes, stirring all the time. Take it off the heat again, pour into a bowl, cover with plastic wrap and chill. When it's cold, whip the cream and fold in. Have a sneaky taste of it—how good?

2 Meanwhile, put the strawberries into a bowl, cover with confectioners' sugar and Cointreau and chill them for about 1 hour. Break the cake up into chunks and either line the bottom of a big glass bowl or divide into six glasses or little bowls. (I like it both ways, but I do love that slurping sound when you spoon a big portion out of a large bowl.) Splash some Cointreau over the cake.

3 Tip the strawberries on top of the cake, then the kiwi slices. Warm the jam with a little water to soften it, then pour it over the cake and fruit. Spoon all the chilled custard onto the cake and fruit.

4 To make the topping, whip the cream and mix with the mascarpone, then spoon over the custard. Finally, sprinkle the toasted coconut on top and serve—you'll never buy a packet dessert again.

14oz strawberries, hulled and chopped into good-sized chunks

½ cup confectioners' sugar

good glugs of Cointreau

9oz cake, pound, jelly roll, muffins—all work well

2 kiwi fruit, peeled and sliced

9oz good quality strawberry jam (say, ¾ jar Bonne Maman)

For the custard

6 egg yolks

½ cup + 1 tbsp superfine sugar

5–6 tbsp all-purpose flour

1¾ cups canned coconut milk

seeds of 1 vanilla bean

¾ cup heavy cream

For the topping

½ cup whipping cream

½ cup mascarpone cheese

½ cup desiccated coconut, toasted

Cherry tiramisu cheesecake

Feeds 12

This combines black forest gâteau with a tiramisu, both of which have become a bit corny in recent times, so the only way to rescue them is to turn them into cheesecake!

1 To make the base, put the crackers, butter, and sugar into a bowl and combine well, then press into a 9inch springform pan and chill for 20 minutes.

2 Preheat the oven to 350°F. Drain the cherries and reserve the juice. Put the juice and booze in a small pan and bring to a boil. Combine the cornstarch with a little water to make a paste, then add to the liquid. This will thicken it to a "jam." Cook over low heat for a couple of minutes, then pour over the cherries and stir to combine. Place a few cherries on the cracker base.

3 To make the topping, beat the cheeses together with the sugar and vanilla, then fold in the eggs, one at a time. Finally, stir in the chocolate and pour onto the cracker base. Bake in the oven for 45–60 minutes, until the top is firm yet yielding. Remove and cool.

4 For the sauce, simply mix the water, syrup, and butter into the chocolate.

5 To serve, spoon the rest of the cherries over the top of the cheesecake, cut a big slab, sit it on a plate with choccy sauce and cream and enjoy.

For the base

8oz crushed graham crackers

1¼ sticks + 1 tbsp (11 tbsp) unsalted butter, melted

½ cup soft brown sugar

For the filling

7–8oz can black cherries

splash of Kirsch

a little cornstarch

For the topping

1½lb ricotta cheese

8oz tub mascarpone cheese

⅔ cup superfine sugar

dash of vanilla extract

6 eggs

9oz best-quality dark chocolate (not unsweetened), melted

For the sauce

4 tbsp water

1 tbsp English golden syrup or corn syrup

1 tbsp unsalted butter

5½oz best-quality dark chocolate (not unsweetened), melted

cream, to serve

Zucotto

Remember when you couldn't move for tiramisu on restaurant menus? It always amazed me that this cracking cream- and choccy-filled dessert didn't make it into our psyche then too—maybe now is the time. Spread the word: zucotto is king.

1 Line a 2½ pint round-bottomed bowl or basin with plastic wrap. Mix the brandy, orange liqueur, and orange juice together in a separate bowl and dip the cake slices in it. Line the bowl or basin with three-quarters of the moist cake slices until all the inside is covered.

2 Fold the confectioners' sugar into the cream.

3 Grate half the chocolate and mix with all the nuts and three-quarters of the cream. Spread over the cake slices in the basin, then mold a hollow in the middle.

4 Melt the remaining chocolate and stir into the rest of the cream. Put this in the hollow and smooth.

5 Cover the cream with the remaining moist cake slices, then cover and chill for 24 hours.

6 Turn the cake out onto a plate, pour over some melted chocolate, then cut generous pieces and eat with yet more cream.

3 tbsp brandy

2 tbsp orange liqueur

5 tbsp fresh orange juice

2 shop-bought pound cakes, trimmed and cut into slices

⅞ cup confectioners' sugar

2 cups heavy cream, whipped

5½oz best-quality dark chocolate (not unsweetened), melted

½ cup slivered, toasted almonds

½ cup roasted skinned hazelnuts

melted chocolate and cream, to serve

Peanut butter and
jelly cheesecake

This is a real '"love or hate"'recipe; for me the combo is so terrific. Use Skippy supercrunch peanut butter, it has a taste and texture like no other for this recipe.

1 To make the base, put the crackers and butter into a bowl, combine well and press into a 9inch springform pan. Chill for 20 minutes.

2 Preheat the oven to 350ºF. For the topping, just put the cheese, sugar, eggs, and vanilla into a blender and pulse until smooth. Don't worry if the mix seems a bit runny, the eggs will set it.

3 Spoon the mixture into a bowl and fold in the peanut butter.

4 Spread the jam over the cracker base, leaving about a 1inch gap all the way round, then spoon the peanut mixture on top.

5 Bake in the oven for about 1 hour. The cheesecake should be springy and just set in the middle. If you can turn off the oven and leave the cake in with the door just open until cool, this will help to stop it cracking, but it's not crucial as it'll get eaten straight away once it's cool.

For the base

7oz crushed graham crackers

$1\frac{1}{4}$ sticks + 1 tbsp (11 tbsp) unsalted butter, melted

For the topping

$2\frac{1}{2}$ cups full-fat cream cheese

$\frac{2}{3}$ cup superfine sugar

6 eggs

splash of vanilla extract

$\frac{2}{3}$ cup crunchy peanut butter

$\frac{2}{3}$ cup strawberry jam

Litchi and toasted coconut cheesecake

Feeds 12

As you know, I love Asian food, but their lack of dairy makes the desserts a bit disappointing for Western palates, so this member of my cheesecake family uses lovely Asian influences in our favorite dessert. This is lovely served with mango kulfi or lime sorbet.

1 Usual base job: combine the crackers, sugar, and butter. Press into a 9inch springform pan and chill for 20 minutes.

2 Preheat the oven to 350°F. Put the coconut under a hot broiler and shake around until it's toasted and golden. Don't even think about leaving it as I guarantee you'll burn it—I always do and so do my team.

3 Put the cheese and sugar into a food processor and pulse together, then add the eggs and pulse to combine.

4 Tip the mixture into a large bowl and fold in the litchis and 1 cup of the coconut. Spoon onto the cracker base, then sprinkle over the remaining coconut.

5 Bake in the oven for about 1 hour. You're looking for a cake that's firm yet yielding! Allow to cool before serving.

For the base

9oz crushed graham crackers

½ cup soft light brown sugar

1¼ sticks + 1 tbsp (11 tbsp) unsalted butter, melted

For the filling

2 cups desiccated coconut

2lb cream cheese

⅔ cup superfine sugar

6 eggs

15oz can of litchis, drained, or 12 fresh, peeled and pitted

More chocolate than is good for you

I recommend you make this for someone you fancy—wife, husband, girlfriend, lover, Britney Spears. As long as they love choccy, I guarantee they will be powerless to your advances as the cupid of cheesecakes takes control.

1 Crush the bourbon biscuits, add the butter and mix well, then press into a 9inch springform pan and chill for 20 minutes.

2 Preheat the oven to 350°F. To make the filling, put the chocolate in a bowl over barely simmering water (make sure the water doesn't touch the bottom of the bowl) and leave until melted.

3 Put the cream cheese and superfine sugar in a food processor and whiz until smooth, then add the eggs and pulse to mix. Add the cocoa powder and melted chocolate and pulse again.

4 Spoon the filling onto the cracker base and bake in the oven for about 1 hour until springy to the touch. Allow to cool in the pan then turn it out.

5 Ideally this should be served topped with grated chocolate, a dusting of cocoa powder and with a rich chocolate sauce. To make the sauce, melt the chocolate and cream over a bowl of simmering water, then whisk in the butter. (Serve the sauce immediately as it won't reheat.) Now wait for the magic to work.

For the base

9oz British bourbon (or Oriels) biscuits

1 stick + 1 tbsp (9 tbsp) unsalted butter, melted

For the filling

7oz best-quality dark chocolate (not unsweetened)

2lb full-fat cream cheese

2/3 cup superfine sugar

6 eggs

3/4 cup cocoa powder, plus extra for dusting

For the sauce

8oz best-quality dark chocolate (not unsweetened), plus extra for sprinkling

1 cup heavy cream

2 tbsp unsalted butter, cut into small pieces

Goat's cheese and lemon cheesecake

Feeds 12

This is a brilliant dessert for anyone without a hugely sweet tooth, the strong goat's cheese works brilliantly with the lemon; it's the only slightly grown-up one of all the cheesecakes.

1 To make the base, put the crackers, nuts, and butter into a bowl, mix together and press into a 9inch springform pan. Chill for 20 minutes.

2 Preheat the oven to 350°F. Pop both cheeses and the sugar into a food processor and pulse till smoothish. I like a bit of texture in this one.

3 Add the eggs and lemon zest and juice and pulse to combine, then spoon onto the cracker base. Bake in the oven for about 1 hour until the cake is springy. Let it cool fully before turning out. I like to serve this with Greek yogurt, rather than cream.

For the base

7oz crushed graham crackers

½ cup crushed pecans

1 stick + 1 tbsp (9 tbsp) unsalted butter, melted

For the filling

1lb 5oz peeled goat's cheese

10oz mascarpone cheese

⅔ cup superfine sugar

6 eggs

zest and juice of 2 lemons

Pecan and white chocolate pie

Feeds 12

While I love the sophistication of a classic lemon tart and the delights of summer fruits, I think a piece of pie is second only to cheesecake in the dessert stakes. Pecan pie is a sugar junkies' delight. To make it richer I'm adding white chocolate.

1 Preheat the oven to 400°F. Roll out the pastry on a lightly floured surface and press it into a 10inch tart case. Line the pastry with foil and rice or baking beans and bake in the oven for 15 minutes. Then remove the rice and foil and cook for another 15 minutes to dry out the case.

2 Beat one of the eggs and brush the pastry case with this eggwash, then cook for a further 5 minutes to seal the case.

3 Meanwhile, make the filling. Whisk the remaining eggs well, then add the sugar, syrup, butter, and vanilla and mix well.

4 Lightly break half the nuts and fold into the mixture, together with the chocolate. Pour the mix into the cooked case and then top with the remaining nuts.

5 Reduce the oven to 350°F and bake the pie for 40 minutes until set (don't panic if the mixture looks too sloppy—it will set it fast). Leave the pie to cool.

6 Serve a large wedge with a spoonful of wicked whipped cream.

1 quantity of sweet shortcrust pastry (see page 124)
flour for dusting
7 eggs
1 packed cup soft light brown sugar
$\frac{1}{2}$ cup English golden syrup or corn syrup
2oz unsalted butter, melted
a dash of vanilla extract
1lb shelled pecan nuts
$3\frac{1}{2}$oz white chocolate, grated
whipped cream, to serve

Passion fruit tart

Feeds 8–10

If you like classic French lemon tart, then you're gonna love this baby. The exotic taste of passion fruit is magnificent. In fact, the passion fruit syrup is a great sweet sauce for ice creams and poured over fruit.

1 To make the pastry, put the flour, butter, salt, and confectioners' sugar in a food processor and pulse until "crumby." Add the milk and egg yolks and pulse until it forms a dough. Turn it out onto a floured surface and knead for a few minutes, then cover and chill for at least 1 hour.

2 Turn the pastry out onto your floured surface and roll out 2inches larger than a 11inch tart case. Push the pastry into the base, leaving the excess hanging over the sides, and chill for at least 30 minutes.

3 Preheat the oven to 350°F. Line the pastry case with foil and rice or baking beans and bake in the oven for 20 minutes. Remove the rice or beans and foil, brush with the eggwash and cook for a further 10 minutes. Remove from the oven and trim off the excess pastry with a sharp knife. Leave to cool.

4 To make the filling, put the sugar and water into a pan and heat gently until the sugar dissolves. Tip in the passion fruit pulp and allow to cool.

5 Whisk the eggs and sugar together, then add the cream. Using a slotted spoon, add all the passion fruit pulp to the cream mixture with a little of the juice, probably about 1 tablespoon. Reserve the remaining juice to use as extra sauce.

6 Pour this custard into the cooked and cooled tart case. Incidentally, a little tip is to fill the tart case while it's sitting on the oven shelf, with the shelf pulled out—genius or what?

7 Reduce the oven to 325°F and bake the tart on the middle shelf for about 40 minutes. It should still be a little wobbly, but it will carry on cooking and will set. To serve, dust the tart with confectioners' sugar and a spoonful of the extra sauce.

For the pastry

$1\frac{3}{4}$ cups all-purpose flour, plus extra for dusting

$\frac{3}{4}$ stick (6 tbsp) cold unsalted butter, cubed

pinch of salt

$\frac{7}{8}$ cup confectioners' sugar, sifted

$3\frac{1}{2}$ tbsp milk

2 egg yolks

1 egg, beaten, for eggwash

confectioners' sugar, to serve

For the filling

$1\frac{3}{4}$ cups superfine sugar

$\frac{2}{3}$ cup water

pulp and juice of 12 passion fruit

9 eggs

$1\frac{1}{4}$ cups heavy cream

Chocolate and prune tart with Earl Grey tea custard

Feeds at least 8

If you think prunes are something to be avoided at all costs, think again, at least until you've tried this decadent tart. Soaking them in Earl Grey tea overnight brings out a really rich flavor in them, which goes particularly well with chocolate—and brandy.

1 Preheat the oven to 400°F. Roll out the pastry on a lightly floured surface and press it into a 10inch tart case. Line the pastry with foil and rice or baking beans and bake in the oven for 15 minutes. Then remove the rice and foil and cook for another 15 minutes to dry out the case.

2 Brush the pastry case with the eggwash, then cook for a further 5 minutes to seal the case.

3 To make the filling, strain the prunes and reserve the tea.

4 Put the chocolate and butter into a bowl.

5 Pour the cream into a pan and bring just up to a boil, then pour over the chocolate and butter and stir until it's all smooth and creamy.

6 Pour just enough of the chocolate mixture into the pastry case to leave a little space at the top, then press the prunes into the surface in a jolly attractive manner. Chill to set.

7 To make the custard, heat the milk to scalding point.

8 Whisk the egg yolks and sugar together in a pan, then pour the milk over them and stir to combine. Add the vanilla seeds and about 4 tbsp of the reserved Earl Grey tea and put back on a low heat. Cook, stirring, until the custard will coat the back of a spoon.

9 Cut a big fat piece of tart, sit it on a plate, pour on some custard and have a large brandy.

1 quantity sweet shortcrust pastry (see page 124)
flour for dusting
1 egg, beaten, for eggwash

For the filling

20 Agen prunes, pitted and soaked in Earl Grey tea overnight
10oz best-quality dark chocolate (not unsweetened), broken into pieces
2 tbsp unsalted butter
$1\frac{1}{4}$ cups heavy cream

For the custard

$1\frac{3}{4}$ cups milk
4 egg yolks
2 tbsp superfine sugar
seeds of 1 vanilla bean

Steamed suet pudding with banana and toffee

This is a real, old-fashioned British pudding. It stirs memories for the "old folks" and the curiosity of their grandchildren. My version is like that long-lost friend who was a bit geeky at school, but has grown into a smooth sophisticated professional and is now everyone's best mate. Go on, you know you want to...

1 Put the flour, baking powder, suet, sugar, currants, and orange zest into a bowl and stir to mix. Add the milk and bananas and mix to a dough.

2 Roll the dough into a cylinder, about 6 x 2inches. Wrap in buttered greaseproof, leaving room for it to rise, and seal at each end. Put into a steamer and steam for 1 hour.

3 To make the custard, put the milk and vanilla seeds into a pan and bring to a boil. Pour onto the egg yolks and sugar and beat well. Return to the pan and cook over a low heat until it coats the back of a spoon.

4 For the toffee sauce, put the sugar, butter, and syrup into a pan and bring to the boil, then remove from the heat and add the cream.

5 Unwrap the steamed pudding and cut into slices. Cover with the custard and then the toffee sauce.

2½ cups all-purpose flour

2 tsp baking powder

5½oz shredded vegetable suet

6 tbsp superfine sugar

1 cup currants

zest of 1 orange

⅔ cup milk

1–2 bananas, chopped

butter for greasing

For the custard

2½ cups milk

seeds of 1 vanilla bean

6 egg yolks

6 tbsp superfine sugar

For the toffee sauce

½ cup soft dark brown sugar

¾ stick + 1 tbsp (7 tbsp) unsalted butter

⅓ cup British golden syrup or corn syrup

1½ cup heavy cream

Melting chocolate pudding

Feeds 4

I feel it my duty to issue a health warning with this magnificent dessert—OK, you have to be willing to experience rich banana cake, melting ganache (the stuff in the middle of posh chocolates) as well as creamy, chocolatey custard. This pud is so sexy that if it was a girlfriend you wouldn't take it home to meet your parents! Speaking of which —the banana loaf recipe is my mom's and is brilliant sliced and buttered on its own. Thanks, mom.

1 First make the ganache. Put the chocolate and butter in a bowl. Pour the cream into a pan, add the sugar and bring to a boil, then pour over the chocolate and butter and stir to melt. Cover and chill for at least 4 hours.

2 Preheat the oven to 350°F. Grease a 2lb loaf tin. To make the banana loaf, dissolve the bicarbonate of soda in the milk, then add the bananas. Sift the baking powder and flour together in a large bowl, then fold in the banana mixture. Stir in the butter, sugars, and the eggs. Spoon the mixture into the loaf pan and bake for about 1 hour, until set. Allow to cool.

3 To make the custard, put the chocolate, coffee, and butter into a bowl. In a separate bowl, whisk together the eggs, egg yolks, and sugar. Put the cream and milk into a saucepan, bring to a boil, then pour over the chocolate and coffee mixture and stir to melt. Then pour this over the whisked eggs and sugar and stir to combine.

4 Trim the edges of the banana loaf and cut the loaf into 1inch cubes. Put the cubes in a large bowl, pour enough chocolate custard over to cover them, and leave to stand for 30 minutes.

5 Preheat the oven to 400°F. Butter four rings, 3inch ideally, and stand them on waxed paper. Pack each halfway with some of the custardy cake. Roll a ball of ganache and pop it onto the middle of the cake, top with more cake and a little more custard. Bake for 15 minutes and serve immediately with the remaining custard or cream. When you cut open the pud the melted ganache will ooze out.

For the banana loaf

1 tsp bicarbonate of soda

2 tbsp milk

3 mashed bananas

1 tsp baking powder

1¾ cups all-purpose flour

1 stick + 1 tbsp (9 tbsp) unsalted butter, softened

⅓ cup brown sugar

½ cup granulated sugar

2 eggs, beaten

For the custard

9oz best-quality dark chocolate (not unsweetened), broken into pieces

a shot of strong espresso coffee

½ stick (4 tbsp) unsalted butter

3 eggs and 2 yolks

¾ cup brown sugar

1¼ cups heavy cream

¾ cup milk

For the ganache

9oz best-quality dark chocolate (not unsweetened), broken into pieces

1 tbsp butter

1 cup heavy cream

2 tbsp superfine sugar

Chocolate brownies
with marshmallow sauce

Feeds 4

Are they a cake or a cookie? I can never decide, so I constantly eat them to try and make up my mind. These fellas are really rich and the melty, marshmallow sauce is like eating liquid fluffy clouds.

1 Preheat the oven to 350°F. Put the eggs and sugar in a bowl and beat until pale and creamy, then add the butter.

2 Sift the flour and cocoa into the egg mixture, then add the melted choccy and the nuts and mix well.

3 Spoon the mixture into a greased 8inch baking dish and bake in the oven for about 35 minutes. Allow to cool.

4 To make the sauce, bring the cream and vanilla to a boil, then simmer for 5 minutes to thicken. Now stir in the marshmallows. The sauce is ready when the marshmallows are half melted.

5 Cut a decent chunk of brownie and pour over the liquid clouds!

4 eggs

1 cup superfine sugar

2 stick (1 cup) unsalted butter, melted, plus extra for greasing

⅔ cup all-purpose flour

¾ cup cocoa powder

8oz best-quality dark chocolate (not unsweetened), melted

1 cup chopped skinned hazelnuts

For the sauce

¾ cup heavy cream

seeds of 1 vanilla pod

4oz pink marshmallows

Hot choccy and churros

Gives salvation to 6

This makes me think of Spain—Valencia in particular. After a particularly heavy night, which ended up in an open-air salsa club by the marina, I struggled round the corner to get a sugary fix of churros, the sweet donut-like icons, together with the sweetest, bestest hot chocolate in the history of the world (it was that big a hangover). So mark this page under "hangover cure" and enjoy.

1 To make the churros, sift the flour, bicarbonate of soda, and salt into a bowl. Make a well in the center, add the water and whisk hard to combine and get rid of any lumps. Let the batter rest for 1 hour.

2 Heat the oil until a piece of bread sizzles when dropped in. Put the batter in a pastry bag and squeeze down into the oil, cutting off after each 4inches of batter. Fry until golden brown, then drain on paper towels and roll the churros in sugar.

3 To make the hot choccy, put the chocolate in a bowl over barely simmering water (make sure the water doesn't touch the bottom of the bowl), and leave until melted.

4 Put the milk and cinnamon stick in a pan and warm for about 10 minutes. Meanwhile, whip the cream. Remove the cinnamon stick and whisk in the melted chocolate and the condensed milk until smooth. Pour into a mug, top with the whipped cream and drink with the churros.

For the churros

$3\frac{1}{4}$ cups all-purpose flour

1 tsp bicarbonate of soda

pinch of salt

$1\frac{3}{4}$ cups boiling water

vegetable oil for deep-frying

superfine sugar for dusting

For the hot choccy

9oz best-quality dark chocolate (not unsweetened), broken into pieces

$1\frac{3}{4}$ cups milk

1 cinnamon stick

1 cup sweetened condensed milk

1 cup whipping cream

Chocolate and red wine pots with donuts

Feeds 8

Even though we've got donuts with them, this is quite a grown-up taste, because of the wine in the choccy pots. The dessert is very rich, so don't serve these after a hugely stodgy meal, but if you do maybe make 16 mini pots and loads of tiny donuts.

1 First make the donuts. Cream the butter and sugar together in a bowl, add the eggs and beat well, then add a dash of vanilla extract and the milk.

2 In a separate bowl, mix the flour, polenta, baking powder, and a pinch of salt. Add to the creamed ingredients and mix well. Sprinkle with flour, cover and chill for at least 8 hours.

3 To make the choccy pots, pour the wine into a pan, add ½ cup of the sugar and bring to a boil. Simmer and reduce by two-thirds, then let it cool.

4 Melt the chocolate in a bowl over simmering water, then whisk in the wine syrup followed by the egg yolks.

5 Heat the milk, cream, and remaining sugar in a pan to scalding point, then whisk into the chocolate mixture. Whisk in the butter, pour into eight ramekins and chill until set.

6 Turn out the donut dough onto a floured surface and roll out to ½inch thickness. Using a 5cm/2inch cutter, cut out loads of rounds. Put onto a board, sprinkle with flour and chill for 30 minutes.

7 Heat the oil and deep-fry the donuts until golden brown. Drain on paper towels, then roll them in sugar. Serve alongside the choccy pots with a quenelle of whipped cream, if you like.

For the donuts

¾ stick (6 tbsp) unsalted butter, softened

6 tbsp superfine sugar, plus extra to roll the donuts in

4 eggs

vanilla extract

2 tbsp milk

6 cups all-purpose flour, plus extra for dusting

¾ cup dry polenta

2 tbsp baking powder

salt

vegetable oil for frying

For the choccy pots

1 cup red wine, medium bodied and fruity

⅔ cup superfine sugar

1lb 2oz best-quality dark chocolate (not unsweetened), broken into pieces

8 egg yolks

1 cup + 1–2 tbsp, if necessary, milk

1 cup heavy cream

1 tbsp unsalted butter

whipped cream, to serve (optional)

Strawberry samosas

Feeds 6

These are good fun and great to serve after a curry. You can use any soft fruit for the filling—mango also works particularly well. If you don't fancy them with yogurt, just drizzle with some honey.

1 To make the pastry, sift the flour and salt into a bowl, then "cut" the butter into it until combined. Add the milk and form into a dough, then cover and chill for 20 minutes.

2 For the filling, put the strawberries into a bowl, add the lemon zest, sugar, and cinnamon and stir to combine.

3 Roll out the pastry on a lightly floured surface and cut into six circles. Cut each circle in half and place a little of the strawberry mixture in one corner then fold over the opposite corner to make a tight triangle. Press down the edges to seal and brush with a little butter.

4 Heat the oil and shallow-fry the samosas until crisp and golden on all sides.

5 To make the yogurt dressing, simply combine the yogurt and mint in a bowl.

6 For the basil syrup, put the sugar, water and vanilla in a pan and heat until the sugar has dissolved. Allow to cool, then put in a food processor with the basil and blitz, then pass through a very fine strainer.

7 Serve a couple of samosas with a dollop of yogurt dressing and a swirl of basil syrup.

1¾ cups all-purpose flour, plus extra for dusting

pinch of salt

2 tbsp unsalted butter, plus extra for brushing

2 tbsp warm milk

vegetable oil for shallow frying

For the filling

8oz strawberries, hulled and chopped

zest of ½ lemon

⅓ cup soft light brown sugar

pinch of cinnamon

For the yogurt dressing

¾ cup Greek yogurt

lots of freshly chopped mint

For the basil syrup

1 cup superfine sugar

⅔ cup water

splash of vanilla extract

lots of fresh basil leaves

Bounty profiteroles

Feeds 6–8

I like to serve one large profiterole, which is probably really a choux bun, but you can do lots of little ones if you like. Oh, before you start this, you have to make the custard for the filling a day in advance—so none until tomorrow, then.

1 First make the filling. Whisk the egg yolks and sugar in a bowl until pale and fluffy, then sift in the flour and mix well. Pour the coconut milk into a pan and bring to a boil. As soon as it boils, pour it onto the egg mixture and stir well. Pour it back into the pan and bring back to a boil, then turn down the heat and cook for another 5 minutes until it thickens. Spoon it back into a bowl and fold in the desiccated coconut, then cover and chill overnight. Make sure the plastic wrap is resting on the surface so you don't get a skin.

2 The next day, whip the cream and fold into the custard.

3 To make the choux buns, preheat the oven to 400°F. Put the butter and water into a pan, bring to a boil and heat until the butter melts. Take the pan off the heat, tip in all the flour and mix well. Using a wooden spoon, beat in the eggs, one at a time. Add a pinch of salt.

4 Transfer the dough to a pastry bag and allow to cool for a few minutes. Now pipe 'blobs' of pastry onto a floured baking sheet. You'll get about 8 squash or golfball size dollops, or as many little ones as you like. The thing to remember is that the pastry will at least double in size, so give them plenty of space on the sheet to expand.

5 Bake in the oven for 30–40 minutes. You want them golden and firm on the outside and dry in the middle. I quite often put them on the bottom shelf for another 5–10 minutes to make sure.

6 To make the sauce, simply heat the ingredients together in a pan until combined.

7 Make a small hole in the base of each profiterole and pipe in some custard. Then sit it in the middle of a plate and pour over some warm choccy sauce. I think this is where I say it's a taste of paradise.

$1\frac{1}{4}$ sticks + 1 tbsp (11 tbsp) unsalted butter

1 cup water

$1\frac{3}{4}$ cups all-purpose flour, plus extra for dusting

6 eggs

pinch of salt

For the filling

6 egg yolks

$\frac{3}{4}$ cup superfine sugar

5 tbsp all-purpose flour

$1\frac{3}{4}$ cups canned coconut milk

$\frac{2}{3}$ cup desiccated coconut

$\frac{3}{4}$ cup heavy cream

For the sauce

7oz best-quality dark chocolate (not unsweetened), broken into pieces

$\frac{1}{2}$ stick (4 tbsp) unsalted butter

$\frac{2}{3}$ cup water

Winter fruit clafoutis

Feeds 6

Sometimes winter fruits can be a bit temperamental, which is why crisps and pies are good options. Another option is this clafoutis, which is basically fruit soaked in booze, topped with a sweet batter and baked. Of course, you can use summer fruits as well.

1 Put the fruit into a bowl, sprinkle the Malibu over and leave for 30 minutes.

2 Preheat the oven to 400°F. Put the milk, cream, and vanilla seeds in a pan and bring to a boil. Take off the heat and cool slightly.

3 Put the sugar and eggs into a bowl and beat well, then add the flour and salt and stir to mix.

4 Strain in the milk mixture and beat well.

5 Butter a 9 x 10inch dish and sprinkle with sugar. Add the fruit, then pour the batter over.

6 Bake in the oven for 25 minutes, then leave to cool. Serve with lightly whipped cream.

1lb prepared winter fruits, such as cranberry, pear, apple

4 tbsp Malibu coconut liqueur

½ cup milk

⅔ cup whipping cream, plus extra to serve

seeds from 1 vanilla bean

¾ cup superfine sugar, plus extra for sprinkling

4 eggs

3½ tbsp all-purpose flour

pinch of salt

butter for greasing

Blueberry pancakes

Feeds 4–6

Now the cottage cheese in the mixture is wonderful. I started using it because one of my fave authors, Robert Crais, has a detective character called Elvis Cole, who uses cottage cheese in his pancake mix, so I tried it and it works—see what you learn from books.

1 Mix the flour, bicarbonate of soda, and sugar together in a bowl.

2 In a separate bowl, combine the egg, melted butter, milk, and cottage cheese, then stir into the flour mix. Stir in the blueberries and lemon zest.

3 Spoon some of the mixture into a lightly oiled warm skillet and cook for 1 minute on each side, until golden. Continue to make pancakes in the same way with the remaining mixture.

4 Sit a few pancakes in a stack and drizzle maple syrup over the top.

$1\frac{1}{2}$ cups self-rising flour

1 tsp bicarbonate of soda

4 tbsp superfine sugar

1 egg

$\frac{1}{2}$ stick (4 tbsp) unsalted butter, melted

1 cup milk

$\frac{1}{2}$ cup cottage cheese

8oz blueberries

zest of 1 small lemon

vegetable oil for frying

maple syrup, to serve

Banana tarte tatin

I remember sitting in a café in Paris eating warm apple tatin and drinking a brandy with Ali, my wife, and thinking all was right with the world. That's how tatin makes you feel; it's warming, comforting and scrummy—but I prefer dark rum to brandy and bananas go better with my tipple, so I wait for the day when it's banana tatin and rum in a café in Jamaica—or pour my own!

1 Preheat the oven to 375°F. Pour the water into a heavy-bottomed pan, sprinkle over the sugar and heat, without stirring, until the sugar dissolves, then simmer gently until the sugar turns golden. Stir in the butter, then pour into a 7inch round baking pan.

2 Pack the banana pieces tightly into the pan.

3 Press the pastry over the top of the bananas and trim, then bake for about 20 minutes, until the pastry is crisp and golden.

4 Allow to cool until just warm, then turn out and serve with whipped cream.

3½ tbsp water

½ cup superfine sugar

2 tbsp unsalted butter

12 bananas, peeled and cut into 2inch pieces

7oz ready-rolled puff pastry

whipped cream, to serve

Rosemary and olive oil cake
with honeyed figs

Feeds 8

You know when you fancy a bit of cake with your tea or coffee in the afternoon, but you don't want a sticky gooey beast? Well, this Italian cake hits the spot. It's sweet enough to give a boost and a treat, but doesn't overface you. However, if you serve it with the honeyed figs and black pepper ricotta, you're asking for trouble.

1 Preheat the oven to 325°F. Put the eggs and sugar into a food processor and whiz until pale and fluffy.

2 Keep the motor running and drizzle in the oil, then with the mixer on slow add the flour, baking powder, and salt and pulse to incorporate. Turn out into a bowl and fold in the rosemary.

3 Pour into a 10inch greased loaf pan and bake in the oven for 45–50 minutes. Cool, then turn out.

4 For the figs, put the marsala and honey in a small pan and bring to a boil, then quickly coat the figs.

5 For the ricotta, put all the ingredients into a bowl and stir to mix.

6 Serve slices of the cake with the figs, ricotta, and a glass of vin santo or sweet wine.

4 eggs

¾ cup superfine sugar

½ cup extra-virgin olive oil

2½ cups all-purpose flour

1 tbsp baking powder

pinch of salt

finely chopped fresh rosemary, to taste

butter for greasing

For the honeyed figs

3½ tbsp marsala wine

2 tbsp honey

6 figs, halved

For the ricotta

½ cup ricotta cheese

½ cup whipped cream

2 tbsp superfine sugar

black pepper

Lemon, lime, and orange polenta cake

Feeds 10–12

I don't know why this is so gorgeous. I'm not a huge fan of polenta and I'm not a huge fan of "plain" cakes, but this little number with a cup of tea or coffee is divine. It's so moist—traditionally it's done with just lemon, but I love that fruit candy effect of all three citrus fruits. It's also the kind of cake that cake pans were invented for.

1 Preheat the oven to 350ºF. Cream the butter and sugar in a bowl until pale and fluffy, then stir in the almonds.

2 Add the eggs, one at a time, then the vanilla.

3 Stir in the zests and juices, then mix in the polenta, salt, and baking powder.

4 Spoon the mixture into a 12inch greased and floured cake pan and bake for 45–55 minutes until golden and firm. Leave to cool in the pan.

5 Serve on its own or with some mascarpone—and tea or coffee.

4 sticks (2 cups) unsalted butter, plus extra for greasing

$2\frac{1}{3}$ cups superfine sugar

$4\frac{1}{2}$ cups ground almonds

6 eggs

good dash of vanilla extract

zest of 2 lemons, 1 orange and 1 lime

juice of $\frac{1}{2}$ lemon and $\frac{1}{2}$ lime

a quick squeeze of orange juice

$1\frac{1}{3}$ cups polenta

pinch of salt

$1\frac{1}{2}$ tsp baking powder

flour for dusting

Index

arancini 16, 85
Arugula, fig & pecan salad with creamy blue
cheese 36
asparagus
Asparagus, potato & fennel salad with Italian
dressing 30, 31
Rendang shallot & asparagus curry 84
Stilton, asparagus & caramelized shallot roulade
with spicy chutney 95
avocado, Santa Fe Caesar salad 24

banana leaf, Coconut rice in 107
bananas
Banana dhal 49
Banana loaf 128
Banana tarte tatin 138, 139
Steamed suet pudding with banana & toffee 127
Basic tomato sauce 107
Basil roulade with goat's cheese & sun-blushed
tomatoes 96, 97
Basil syrup 133
beans
Black bean & eggplant chili 88
Italian bean casserole 85
Pumpkin enchiladas with mole sauce 47
Santa Fe Caesar salad 24
see also fava beans; fine green beans
beets
Beet tart 56, 57
caviar 96, 97
Spicy beet & coconut soup 60, 61
Sprouts with beet 103
bell peppers
Blinis with sour cream & roasted bell peppers 11
coleslaw 41
Fattoush 33
Gruyère-filled beefsteak tomatoes 50, 51
Lentils with lemon 102
Panzanella 26, 27
red bell pepper sauce 69
Roasted red bell peppers with fennel 52
salsa 64
Savory Paris-Brest 65
Spicy red bell pepper hummus 12, 13
Stuffed pimentos with thyme & basil 104, 105
Sweet potato & pineapple sandwich 70, 71
Black bean & eggplant chili 88
Blinis with sour cream & roasted bell peppers 11
Blueberry pancakes 136, 137
Bounty profiteroles 134
bread
Coriander seed flat bread 12, 13
Feta cheese bread 10
pizza bases 46
bread (as ingredient)
Cheese sausages 72
Eggplant "stack" with pesto 42
Fattoush 33
Goat's cheese & mango 43
Mushroom "rarebit" on brioche toast 44, 45
Panzanella 26, 27
broccoli, Beet tart 56, 57
brownies, Chocolate, with marshmallow sauce 129

Bubble & squeak 100
butternut squash see pumpkin

cabbage, coleslaws 32, 41
Caesar salad, Santa Fe 24
cakes
Banana loaf 128
Lemon, lime, & orange polenta 141
Rosemary & olive oil, with honeyed figs 140
cannelloni, Goat's cheese, with cherry tomatoes 78
Caramelized onion & mustard tart 92, 93
carrots
Glazed, with caraway seeds 103
Italian bean casserole 85
Peas & carrots 53
spicy coleslaw 32
caviar, beet 96, 97
Celeriac & potato dauphinoise 104
cheese
Arugula, fig & pecan salad with creamy blue cheese 36
Blueberry pancakes 136, 137
Celeriac & potato dauphinoise 104
Four-cheese & zucchini penne 82
Fried halloumi with lemon & capers 14
Gruyère-filled beefsteak tomatoes 50, 51
Hazelnut & mushroom parcels 69
Leek & potato rosti with "rarebit" topping 55
Linguine with potato & pesto 75
Macaroni cheese 74
Mushroom "rarebit" on brioche toast 44, 45
Pan haggerty 100, 101
Parmesan-roasted parsnips 106
Phyllo strudel with port wine sauce 66, 67
Rosemary & olive oil cake with honeyed figs 140
sauce 74
sausages 72
Stilton, asparagus & caramelized shallot roulade
with spicy chutney 95
Stuffed pimentos with thyme & basil 104, 105
Wild mushroom pancakes 68
see also cheesecakes; feta cheese; goat's cheese;
mascarpone; mozzarella
cheesecakes
Cherry tiramisu 115
Goat's cheese & lemon 122
Litchi & toasted coconut 119
More chocolate than is good for you 120, 121
Peanut butter & jelly 118
Cheese sausages with mustard mash & onion gravy 72
chickpeas (garbanzo beans)
Coronation chickpeas & potato salad 29
Moroccan spaghetti 80, 81
Oriental pie 91
Spicy red bell pepper hummus 12, 13
chili, Black bean & eggplant 88
Chinese mushroom pancakes 48
chocolate
Black bean & eggplant chili 88
Cherry tiramisu cheesecake 115
Chocolate & prune tart with Earl Grey tea custard 126
Chocolate & red wine pots with donuts 132
Chocolate brownies with marshmallow sauce 129
ganache 128
Hot choccy & churros 130, 131
Melting chocolate pudding 128
mole sauce 47

More chocolate than is good for you 120, 121
Pecan & white chocolate pie 123
sauces 115, 120, 128, 134
Zucotto 116, 117
choux pastry 65, 134
churros 130, 131
chutneys 56, 95
clafoutis, Winter fruit 135
coconut & coconut milk
Bounty profiteroles 134
Coconut rice in banana leaf 107
Curry sauce 70, 71
Jerk-spiced pumpkin pie 94
Litchi & toasted coconut cheesecake 119
Red Thai bean curry 86, 87
Rendang shallot & asparagus curry 84
Spicy beet & coconut soup 60, 61
Strawberry & coconut trifle 114
coleslaw 32, 41
Coriander seed flat bread 12, 13
Coronation chickpeas & potato salad 29
cucumber
Chinese mushroom pancakes 48
Fattoush 33
Pickled cucumber salad 30
Tzatziki 21
Watermelon salad 36
curry
Eggplant tikka masala 83
pastes 84, 86
Plantain & mango 90
Red Thai bean 86, 87
Rendang shallot & asparagus 84
sauces 70, 83, 94
custard sauces 114, 126, 127, 128

dauphinoise, Celeriac & potato 104
dhal, Banana 49
Dolmades 21
donuts 132
churros 130, 131
dressings 14, 24, 32, 33, 36, 50, 53, 54
Italian 25
nuoc cham 34, 35

eggplant
Black bean & eggplant chili 88
Eggplant "roll-mops" 40
Eggplant "stack" with pesto 42
Eggplant tikka 41
Eggplant tikka masala 83
Griddled eggplant salad with nuoc cham 34, 35
Savory Paris-Brest 65
eggs
Huevos rancheros 64
Ojja with sweet potato & okra 89
Sun-blush Niçoise 25
see also recipes normally made with eggs
(eg custard sauces)

Fattoush 33
fava beans
Favetta 15
Ojja with sweet potato & okra 89
Red Thai bean curry 86, 87
Favetta 15

fennel
    Arugula, fig & pecan salad with creamy blue cheese 36
    Asparagus, potato & fennel salad with
        Italian dressing 30, 31
    Lemon, fennel & oyster mushroom salad 37
    Roasted red bell peppers with fennel 52
feta cheese
    Feta cheese bread 10
    Warm stack of Greek salad with parsley pesto 28
    Watermelon salad 36
figs
    Arugula, fig & pecan salad with creamy blue cheese 36
    Rosemary & olive oil cake with honeyed figs 140
fine green beans
    Fine green beans with garlic & tomato sauce 106
    Green papaya salad 37
    Red Thai bean curry 86, 87
    Sun-blush Niçoise 25
Four-cheese & zucchini penne 82
Fried halloumi with lemon & capers 14
fruit
    Winter fruit clafoutis 135
    see also specific fruits (eg strawberries)

ganache, chocolate 128
garbanzo beans see chickpeas
Glazed carrots with caraway seeds 103
Gnocchi with wild mushroom & rosemary ragu 76, 77
goat's cheese
    Basil roulade with goat's cheese & sun-blushed
        tomatoes 96, 97
    Beet tart 56, 57
    Goat's cheese & lemon cheesecake 122
    Goat's cheese & mango 43
    Goat's cheese cannelloni with cherry tomatoes 78
    Savory Paris-Brest 65
granita, Strawberry, vodka & black pepper 112
grape leaves, Dolmades 21
gravy, Onion 72
Greek salad, Warm stack of, with parsley pesto 28
green beans see fava beans; fine green beans
Green papaya salad 37
Griddled eggplant salad with nuoc cham 34, 35
Gruyère-filled beefsteak tomatoes 50, 51

halloumi, Fried, with lemon & capers 14
Hazelnut & mushroom parcels 69
Honeycomb ice cream 111
Hot choccy & churros 130, 131
Huevos rancheros (ranch eggs) 64
hummus, Spicy red bell pepper 12, 13

ice cream, Honeycomb 111
Italian bean casserole 85
Italian dressing 25

Jerk-spiced pumpkin pie 94

kiwi fruit, Strawberry & coconut trifle 114

leeks
    Leek & potato rosti with "rarebit" topping 55
    Leeks wrapped in phyllo 54
    Phyllo strudel with port wine sauce 66, 67
Lemon, fennel & oyster mushroom salad 37
Lemon grass risotto with lime leaf tapenade 79

Lemon, lime & orange polenta cake 141
lentils
    Banana dhal 49
    Lentils with lemon 102
lettuce
    Fattoush 33
    Santa Fe Caesar salad 24
    Sun-blush Niçoise 25
Lime leaf tapenade 79
Linguine with potato & pesto 75
Litchi & toasted coconut cheesecake 119

Macaroni cheese 74
mango
    Goat's cheese & mango 43
    Plantain & mango curry 90
marshmallow sauce 129
mascarpone
    Cherry tiramisu cheesecake 115
    Four-cheese & zucchini penne 82
    Goat's cheese & lemon cheesecake 122
    Linguine with potato & pesto 75
    Strawberry & coconut trifle 114
    Strawberry soup 112, 113
Melting chocolate pudding 128
mole sauce 47
Moroccan spaghetti 80, 81
mozzarella
    arancini 16, 85
    Eggplant "stack" with pesto 42
    Proper pizza 46
    Roasted red bell peppers with fennel 52
    Sun-dried tomato, mozzarella & basil tart 59
    Tomato & mozzarella cakes 16
    Wild mushroom pancakes 68
mushrooms
    Chinese mushroom pancakes 48
    Gnocchi with wild mushroom & rosemary ragu 76, 77
    Gruyère-filled beefsteak tomatoes 50, 51
    Hazelnut & mushroom parcels 69
    Lemon, fennel & oyster mushroom salad 37
    Mushroom "rarebit" on brioche toast 44, 45
    Oriental pie 91
    Phyllo strudel with port wine sauce 66, 67
    Wild mushroom pancakes 68

nectarines, Strawberry soup 112, 113
Norimaki sushi rolls 18, 19
nuoc cham 34, 35

okra
    Ojja with sweet potato & okra 89
    Sweet potato & pineapple sandwich 70, 71
onions
    Caramelized onion & mustard tart 92, 93
    chutney 56
    Onion gravy 72
    Pickled 40
Oriental pie 91
oyster mushrooms
    Chinese mushroom pancakes 48
    Lemon, fennel & oyster mushroom salad 37

Pan haggerty 100, 101
pancakes
    Blinis with sour cream & roasted bell peppers 11

Blueberry 136, 137
Chinese mushroom 48
Wild mushroom 68
Panzanella 26, 27
papaya salad, Green 37
Parmesan-roasted parsnips 106
parsley pesto 28
parsnips, Parmesan-roasted 106
passion fruit
    Passion fruit tart 124, 125
    Strawberry soup 112, 113
pasta
    Four-cheese & zucchini penne 82
    Goat's cheese cannelloni with cherry tomatoes 78
    Linguine with potato & pesto 75
    Macaroni cheese 74
    Moroccan spaghetti 80, 81
    Penne all'arabiata 73
pastes, curry 84, 86
pastry
    choux 65, 134
    shortcrust 56, 92
    sweet shortcrust 124
pastry dishes
    Bounty profiteroles 134
    Hazelnut & mushroom parcels 69
    Jerk-spiced pumpkin pie 94
    Leeks wrapped in phyllo 54
    Phyllo strudel with port wine sauce 66, 67
    Savory Paris-Brest 65
    Strawberry samosas 133
    see also tarts
Patatas bravas 20
peanut balls, Sticky rice & 15
Peanut butter & jelly cheesecake 118
pears
    chutney 95
    Winter fruit clafoutis 135
Peas & carrots 53
pecans
    Arugula, fig & pecan salad with creamy blue cheese 36
    Pecan & white chocolate pie 123
    Wild mushroom pancakes 68
penne
    Four-cheese & zucchini penne 82
    Penne all'arabiata 73
pesto 42, 75
    parsley pesto 28
Phyllo
    Leeks wrapped in phyllo 54
    Phyllo strudel with port wine sauce 66, 67
Pickled cucumber salad 30
Pickled onions 40
pies
    Jerk-spiced pumpkin 94
    Oriental 91
    Pecan & white chocolate 123
pimentos see bell peppers
pineapple sandwich, Sweet potato & 70, 71
pizza, Proper 46
plantain
    Jerk-spiced pumpkin pie 94
    Plantain & mango curry 90
plum sauce 48
polenta
    donuts 132

Lemon, lime & orange polenta cake 141
popsicles 110
port wine sauce 66, 67
potatoes
    Asparagus, potato & fennel salad with
        Italian dressing 30, 31
    Bubble & squeak 100
    Celeriac & potato dauphinoise 104
    Coronation chickpeas & potato salad 29
    Gnocchi with wild mushroom &
        rosemary ragu 76, 77
    Leek & potato rosti with "rarebit" topping 55
    Linguine with potato & pesto 75
    Oriental pie 91
    Pan haggerty 100, 101
    Patatas bravas 20
    Smoky roasties 102
    Sun-blush Niçoise 25
    Thai spiced potato cakes with spicy coleslaw 17
profiteroles, Bounty 134
Proper pizza 46
prunes, Chocolate & prune tart with Earl Grey tea
    custard 126
pumpkin
    Jerk-spiced pumpkin pie 94
    Pumpkin enchilladas with mole sauce 47

ragu, Rosemary 76, 77
Ranch eggs (huevos rancheros) 64
"rarebit"
    Leek & potato rosti with "rarebit" topping 55
    Mushroom "rarebit" on brioche toast 44, 45
raspberries, Strawberry soup 112, 113
red cabbage, spicy coleslaw 32
red peppers see bell peppers
Red Thai bean curry 86, 87
Rendang shallot & asparagus curry 84
rice
    arancini 16, 85
    Coconut rice in banana leaf 107
    Dolmades 21
    Lemon grass risotto with lime leaf tapenade 79
    Norimaki sushi rolls 18, 19
    Ojja with sweet potato & okra 89
    Sticky rice & peanut balls 15
    Tomato & mozzarella cakes 16
Roasted red bell peppers with fennel 52
"roll-mops", Eggplant 40
Rosemary & olive oil cake with honeyed figs 140
Rosemary ragu 76, 77
roulades
    Basil, with goat's cheese & sun-blushed
        tomatoes 96, 97
    Stilton, asparagus & caramelized shallot, with spicy
        chutney 95

salads
    Arugula, fig & pecan, with creamy blue cheese 36
    Asparagus, potato & fennel, with Italian dressing 30, 31
    coleslaws 32, 41
    Coronation chickpeas & potato 29
    Fattoush 33
    Green papaya 37
    Griddled eggplant, with nuoc cham 34, 35
    Lemon, fennel & oyster mushroom 37

Panzanella 26, 27
Pickled cucumber 30
Santa Fe Caesar salad 24
Sun-blush Niçoise 25
Sweet potato 32
Warm stack of Greek salad with parsley pesto 28
Watermelon 36
salsa 64
samosas, Strawberry 133
Santa Fe Caesar salad 24
sauces
    cheese 74
    chocolate 115, 120, 128, 134
    curry 70, 83, 94
    custard 114, 126, 127, 128
    marshmallow 129
    mole 47
    onion gravy 72
    plum 48
    port wine 66, 67
    red bell pepper 69
    toffee 127
    tomato 107
sausages, cheese 72
Savory Paris-Brest 65
shallot & asparagus curry, Rendang 84
shortcrust pastry 56, 92
    sweet 124
Simple tomato tart 58
Smoky roasties 102
soups
    Spicy beet & coconut 60, 61
    Strawberry 112, 113
spaghetti, Moroccan 80, 81
Spicy beet & coconut soup 60, 61
spicy coleslaw 32
Spicy red bell pepper hummus with coriander seed
    flat bread 12, 13
spinach
    Goat's cheese cannelloni with cherry tomatoes 78
    Jerk-spiced pumpkin pie 94
Steamed suet pudding with banana & toffee 127
sprouts
    Bubble & squeak 100
    Sprouts with beet 103
squash see pumpkin
Sticky rice & peanut balls 15
Stilton, asparagus & caramelized shallot roulade with
    spicy chutney 95
strawberries
    Strawberry & black pepper popsicle 110
    Strawberry & coconut trifle 114
    Strawberry samosas 133
    Strawberry soup 112, 113
    Strawberry, vodka & black pepper granita 112
strudel with port wine sauce, Phyllo 66, 67
Stuffed pimentos with thyme & basil 104, 105
Sun-blush Niçoise 25
Sun-dried tomato, mozzarella & basil tart 59
sushi rolls, Norimaki 18, 19
sweet potatoes
    Ojja with sweet potato & okra 89
    Oriental pie 91
    Sweet potato & pineapple sandwich 70, 71
    Sweet potato salad 32

tapenade, Lime leaf 79
tarts
    Banana tarte tatin 138, 139
    Beet 56, 57
    Caramelized onion & mustard 92, 93
    Chocolate & prune, with Earl Grey tea custard 126
    Passion fruit 124, 125
    Pecan & white chocolate pie 123
    Simple tomato 58
    Sun-dried tomato, mozzarella & basil 59
Thai spiced potato cakes with spicy coleslaw 17
tiramisu cheesecake, Cherry 115
toffee sauce 127
tomatoes
    Basic tomato sauce 107
    Basil roulade with goat's cheese & sun-blushed
        tomatoes 96, 97
    Beet tart 56, 57
    Black bean & eggplant chili 88
    Eggplant "stack" with pesto 42
    Eggplant tikka masala 83
    Fattoush 33
    Fine green beans with garlic & tomato sauce 106
    Gnocchi with wild mushroom &
        rosemary ragu 76, 77
    Goat's cheese cannelloni with cherry tomatoes 78
    Green papaya salad 37
    Gruyère-filled beefsteak tomatoes 50, 51
    Italian bean casserole 85
    Macaroni cheese 74
    mole sauce 47
    Moroccan spaghetti 80, 81
    Ojja with sweet potato & okra 89
    Panzanella 26, 27
    Patatas bravas 20
    Penne all'arabiata 73
    Phyllo strudel with port wine sauce 66, 67
    Proper pizza 46
    Red Thai bean curry 86, 87
    Roasted red bell peppers with fennel 52
    salsa 64
    Savory Paris-Brest 65
    Simple tomato tart 58
    Sun-blush Niçoise 25
    Sun-dried tomato, mozzarella & basil tart 59
    Tomato & mozzarella cakes 16
    Warm stack of Greek salad with parsley pesto 28
Tzatziki 21

Warm stack of Greek salad with parsley pesto 28
Watermelon & lime popsicles 110
Watermelon salad 36
Wild mushroom pancakes 68
Winter fruit clafoutis 135

yellow peppers see bell peppers

zucchini
    Four-cheese & zucchini penne 82
    Gruyère-filled beefsteak tomatoes 50, 51
    salsa 64
    Savory Paris-Brest 65
    Warm stack of Greek salad with parsley pesto 28
Zucotto 116, 117